NORMAN REEDUS:
An Unauthorized Biography

TRUE TALES
OF THE
WALKING
DEAD'S
ZOMBIE HUNTER

New York Times Best-selling Author
MARC SHAPIRO

For more information contact:
Riverdale Avenue Books
5676 Riverdale Avenue
Riverdale, NY 10471.

www.riverdaleavebooks.com

Design by www.formatting4U.com
Cover by Scott Carpenter

Digital ISBN 978-1-62601-220-2
Print ISBN 978-1-62601-219-6

First Edition September 2015

THIS BOOK IS DEDICATED TO...

My wife, Nancy who keeps me normal. My daughter, Rachael who keeps me alert. My granddaughter, Lily who keeps me honest. Brent, Robert and Layla who opened the door to the next chapter. Brady who laughs at all my jokes...at least that's what I think she's doing. Fitch who does the best damned version of playing dead I've ever seen. Lori Perkins for fighting the good fight and shielding me from any stray bullets. Mike Kirby...Live from the land of hopes and dreams. All the great writers, artists and musicians who chose to take the chance. Finally to Norman Reedus...the coolest cat on the planet...at least until the next cool cat comes out to play.

TABLE OF CONTENTS

Author's Notes	Third Is The New First	i
Introduction	Is The Head Dead Yet?	vii
One	Mom's A Bunny, Dad's All Business	1
Two	Traveling Shoes	6
Three	Gnarly	12
Four	Under A Bridge	19
Five	Maps For Drowners	25
Six	If You Blinked You Missed Him	31
Seven	Discover Me	34
Eight	Shy Boy Meets Wonder Woman	43
Nine	Norman Kills	49
Ten	Done And Done	58
Eleven	On The Market	62
Twelve	Scars	67
Thirteen	Norman Does Sick	72
Fourteen	I Live For Pain	78
Fifteen	Norman Gets Dead	86
Sixteen	Norman Never Sleeps	94
Seventeen	The House In The Woods	100
Eighteen	Quick Check The Script	108
Nineteen	The Attack Of The Big Bald Head	115
Twenty	Who's That Lady?	120
Twenty-One	Dead 4 You	122
Twenty-Two	Thanks And No Thanks	126
Twenty-Three	Thanks For The Niceness	130
Twenty-Four	Mr. Reedus Goes To Washington	135
Epilogue	From There To Here	138
Filmography		141
Sources		145
About The Author		147
Other Riverdale Books		148

AUTHOR'S NOTES
THIRD IS THE NEW FIRST

Okay here's the quick and dirty of it. Norman Reedus was a last minute addition to the cast of the always daring AMC's latest television series *The Walking Dead* in 2010 just as the gut-munching show was about to launch its inaugural season. He had been auditioning for an existing character but, when that did not pan out, the producers of the show had been so hypnotized by his sullen, introverted and powerful anti-hero ways that they created the role of crossbow master/uber zombie fighter Daryl Dixon literally out of whole cloth and a group of screenwriters fell all over themselves to write for him.

The gods and/or the Hollywood tastemakers (aren't they one and the same?) take a shine to his ability to kick zombie ass, wax loner in the classic Garbo/Easy Rider sense and project a sexual question mark leaning precariously close to gay while basically seeing the world through a jaundiced, albeit ruggedly individual squint that even the most supportive observers of Reedus have often described as the look of a junkie long past his last fix.

But enough of the preliminaries. The bottom line was that Norman Reedus had, on the strength of playing a hard-bitten survivor in a zombie-infested land, risen from the ashes of a resume that was never less than interesting nor more than obscure to become the next hot commodity in aisle seven of the Hollywood Meat Market. And it was not only the horror and geek mags who took notice. The slick monthlies and all branches of mainstream media had also bought in to this sullen but magnetic actor. All the pop culture dots were being connected.

It was time to unleash the literary hounds.

The first of the paperback originals out of the box were slim affairs, ravaging Wikipedia and the first wave of magazine articles for cut and paste quickies that barely squeaked into double page count length. At this point let me make it plain that I am not above cut and paste (or as we refer to it in the business 'research and good journalism') but only as a last resort when nobody is talking on the record or is asking for money to jog their memory. And I have no problem with somebody getting it out there first, even if it's not me.

The reality is that the first book out on a currently hot celebrity does, with rare exception, end up selling the most copies. Second or even third out of the gate? I've been an also ran in a couple of those races and I can honestly say that it was not pretty.

And so my publisher at Riverdale Avenue Books and I were cautiously optimistic one day when we were tossing around ideas and Norman Reedus came up. I had read up on the actor to the point where I could spot nuggets of life experience that had just plain down and out either been ignored completely or glossed over in a sentence. And it went without saying that I was a fan of the show. I sensed that if people could be found who were willing to talk about Reedus, being third out of the box, figuratively speaking, might be the new first. My publisher agreed to the point where she said she would greenlight the book if I could guarantee enough original voices to fill out what had, to that point, become a fairly familiar tale.

Thus was born *Norman Reedus: True Tales of The Walking Dead's Zombie Hunter*, a very unauthorized but very "real" look at the cool cat with the crossbow who dispatches the undead so we can get our television kicks. This is not a spoiler alert but I can tell you this: I did find people. They did talk. And, considering that, in a couple of cases, I literally surprised them with unexpected phone calls from the other side of the country, they were quite cooperative and candid in clueing me to Norman Reedus' life. There was also a lot of 'research and good journalism' thrown in for good measure. Norman Reedus had taken to sudden stardom like a pro and had made himself available to the press seemingly at every turn. Some interviewers went for the lazy and obvious softballs which Norman deftly handled. Those who dug a bit deeper were also rewarded in kind.

But Norman Reedus was nothing if not a difficult fish to land. Especially when it came to pivotal moments in his life. You see Norman has this habit of changing up history to serve his memory of what happened or to just change things up for the sake of drama. Consequently, there are often maddening moments when Norman, or perhaps the journalist chronicling his life, just can't seem to come to a consensus of opinion. This necessitated endless days of cross matching stories, with Norman's quotes usually carrying the day. But there were those moments where consensus went out the window. One pivotal moment ended up having three different versions, two of which were from Norman's lips while the third came from a reliable source who was on the scene when it all came down. The result was that I ran all three versions in an attempt to get the whole, if convoluted, picture.

Another challenge facing this chronicler of all things Reedus is his filmography. Norman has easily done more films than any three flavors of the moment put together. Most of them are obscure in the extreme, went straight to video or some left field European theatrical/festival runs and, if you're counting all the shorts, there is a core list of approximately 50 films, which does not include television and theater appearances. The chances are good that by the time it's time to turn in this manuscript, he will have added another half dozen credits to his list. To say the least, Norman is prolific, or a workaholic or, most likely, both.

And in line with that, compiling Norman's work habits has often resulted in the scratching of head or, quite simply, a 'what the fuck?' moment. A lot of what Norman has done is not all that surprising. When you're first starting out…well you do what is offered. But if you pick any five Norman Reedus obscurities at random, the chances are real good that his on-screen appearance time in all those films will clock in at less than five minutes. Figuring out why he did *The Boondock Saints* and *Pandorum* are no brainers. But, to be perfectly honest, why he chose to play *Sex Toy Delivery Boy* for less than two minutes and ends up getting a blowjob in the largely gay opus *Luster* is beyond me. But I'm sure Norman had a reason. The location made for a good vacation? He was indebted to a loyal friend? He saw the artifice in every part he did? Only Norman knows for sure, so I'll just keep scratching my head.

The occasional vagary of Norman even extended to, at one point, just how old Norman actually was. When chronicling Norman's first acting role in the play *Maps for Drowners*, two people connected to the scene were pretty sure that Norman was no more than 17 or 18. Norman did not help matters when, in a website interview, he said he was in his early 20's at the time but that even he could not be certain. I finally ended the logjam by taking his birthdate and subtracting it from the year *Maps for Drowners* opened. Game, set and age match to Norman.

And then there was the challenge of chronicling Norman's prodigious work habits. The cat really liked to work, so much so that even the most diligent filmographers to this point were having a tough time catching all the bit parts, often very odd cameos and the solid work in things seemingly nobody ever heard of and that few, if any, would ever see. As stated a couple of paragraphs ago, he is a conundrum with a mystery within a mental Rubik's Cube.

But even as I set out to write the book, I knew I could well be on a deadline of sorts and that would ultimately influence how I told the tale. *The Walking Dead* has made its bones largely on the wings of unpredictability. Yes there's the expected zombie gore. There's also a boatload of character. But built into the show is the notion that nice guys don't always make it to FADE OUT and that long-running characters have suddenly and unexpectedly perished. Bottom line, nobody is assured of making it to the grand finale. Not even Daryl.

Consequently a manuscript largely loaded with *Walking Dead* anecdotes and a cursory look at Norman Reedus' backstory would run the risk of being nothing more than a quaint history if it were to come out after Daryl's demise. Which meant heavy on everything leading up to *The Walking Dead* and then sprinkle in as needed. After all, this is a book about Norman Reedus and not a lot of 'minute' on just one role, albeit the role that got him here.

Norman has obviously had a long and diverse career before *The Walking Dead* and will, no doubt, in years to come, ride off into the sunset to bigger and better things. So why not get pop culture, whose members are notorious for being of the moment, caught up?

Finally I can guarantee even those who think they know Norman Reedus like a book will come away from *Norman Reedus: True Tales of The Walking Dead's Zombie Hunter* with stuff that will make you shudder at what some people go through to make it to the top. You've been warned. The truth can be a bitter pill. You won't find a lot of warm and fuzzy here. Shameless star fucking is not where this book is at. Norman Reedus may well be the last of the angry young men.

Because Norman Reedus is definitely his own man.

Marc Shapiro 2015

INTRODUCTION
IS THE HEAD DEAD YET?

In 2005 Norman Reedus was leaving an REM concert in Berlin, Germany. It had been one of those mellow and triumphant nights. Norman had served in the acting shadows for seemingly decades and now, close to entering middle age, had done little that had actually been seen, let alone appreciated. His talents had finally caught up with the filmmakers and tastemakers, beginning with an intellectually stimulating and esoteric stay at The Berlin Film Festival, in which Norman, long known for his awkwardness in big crowds and social situations, mixed easily with filmmakers, artsy intellectuals and musicians. As well as a few friends.

Among the latter, he reconnected with the members of REM with whom he had developed close ties during an appearance in the band's 1995 music video for the single *Strange Currencies* and had ended the night with lead singer Michael Stipe giving Norman a shout out from the stage. It was the perfect ending to a night of good music, good companionship and all the vibes and recognition that went along with being a modern day bohemian, living for the moment and the possibilities that moment might bring.

At the conclusion of the concert, Norman was about to go outside and hail a cab back to his hotel for a meeting with a director. Ever the generous host, Stipe stepped forward and offered Norman the use of his personal driver. Norman got in and the car drove away from the concert hall…

…And pulled out right in front of an oncoming 18 wheel truck.

The impact was immediate, the sound of metal crushing metal and the shattering of glass a noisy, sonic prelude to destruction. In seconds the car was reduced to rubble. A crowd of horrified onlookers gathered, looking at the mangled and bloody Norman splayed out in the roadway. To this day Norman still gets the emotional shakes when he talks about that night, as could be witnessed in a recent conversation with *Q Magazine*. "I remember looking down at my Blackberry just as I went through the car window and out into the street." He would further reconstruct the moment when he recalled in an *Entertainment Weekly* story that he came to on the street to discover a woman picking glass shards off his face.

Norman was transported to nearby Berlin Hospital, his face literally a mass of blood and broken bones. He recalled feeling like Quasimodo from *The Hunchback of Notre Dame*. "I was hideous," he related in a Q interview. "I didn't want anybody to see me like this, not even my mother and my girlfriend."

Surgeons set to work putting his face back together, inserting a Titanium eye socket to replace the one destroyed in the crash and inserting four screws into his nose to help bring his destroyed cartilage around to something resembling its normal shape.

Norman would spend four months in the Berlin Hospital, a German speaking friend, budding filmmaker Christian Alvart was around for translation purposes but, for the most part, Norman was alone in isolation.

Isolation being a state of mind and being a trait he had grown to love.

Norman had always referred to himself as an artist and had played the part with believability and determination. The notion that he might actually be considered an actor had remained repugnant to him for a long time, even when, by the time he stumbled into *The Walking Dead*, he had long been plying that very craft to a modicum of success. But even to this day, his talents as a sculptor, artist and photographer of some underground note have been worn as badges of honor. It would take him some years to relent to the idea that acting could also be a truly creative outlet.

But through it all, Norman had always done a delicate dance with the dark and desolate even as his celebrity star was ascending. He was not somebody who was dour or remorseful, although many in his small inner circle of friends and significant others might let you know that he did have those bleak moments. Although with his breakthrough in *The Walking Dead* he had become fairly at ease with notoriety and sudden celebrity. But in his demeanor he still seemed to be holding out for the pure artistic life.

Even though celebrity was not beating him down, he had grown to become occasionally bemused and sometimes annoyed at the overzealous fan response to his character. He has had to deal with female zombie extras on *The Walking Dead* set making veiled and not-s-veiled sexual overtures while in full horror makeup. And it hasn't stopped there.

"I've had fans of the show follow me home," Reedus reflected in a *Rolling Stone* interview, "And I had one person try to break into my backyard."

But the mania did not seem to have impacted Norman's day to day walk through the life of being Norman. While on set, his security backup appears to run from little to non-existent, with Reedus seemingly at ease or, at best, tolerant of the media and the mania for Daryl. It is an attitude that is equally in evidence when Norman is in New York, his home away from home when not on *The Walking Dead* set. He walks the street like everyman, now recognized but never in his face recognized. He's the doting parent who immediately elevated his son's street cred when he picked him up from school. And in a Hollywood/celebrity world where loyalty is often nothing more than a seven letter world, Norman has quickly proven a *mensch* among men.

Not long after all things *Walking Dead* and Daryl Dixon became the hot new pop culture talking points, Norman, not unexpectedly, was inundated with big time movie offers, one of the biggest being a part in the next George Clooney movie, *Tomorrowland*. There was only one problem, and for Norman, and it proved to be the deal breaker.

"It came down to the fact that I would have to cut my hair really short for the role," he reflected in *Rolling Stone*. "I'm on a show full time and I can't just cut my hair real short out of nowhere. This is my full time job and I'm not going to do anything to jeopardize that."

Nor was he going to suddenly go all Hollywood with his success and become somebody he was not.

In interviews, he has been forthright in saying that he has always been socially awkward and, to this day, is not fond of being in big crowds. "I'm shy," he told *GQ*. "I'm socially awkward. I'm a loner. I'm more of a listener than a talker."

And despite his seemingly engrained beyond redemption image as the ultimate badass, Norman, in conversation with *The New York Post*, was quick to point out that, in real life, nothing could be further from the truth. "I'm this angry, surly, ready to start a fight guy. But the reality is that I'm kind of a pussycat. I'm kind of a wimp. I don't like confrontation at all."

His home away from home when *The Walking Dead* is on location, has been, by choice, an isolated house deep in the woods. When Norman wants to get away from it all, which is again quite often, he will jump on his Triumph, his motorcycle of choice, and ride with rarely a preordained goal in mind. Whether in his studio working on a piece of sculpture, out in the great wide open with camera in hand or taking a break from his full schedule of film and television work, he can be cordial to co-workers and amazingly forthcoming to his growing legion of fans. He's done the television talk show circuit and by all reports, has proven himself quite adept with happy talk and softball questions. On the personal front, Norman is reportedly the ideal father when he's with his son Mingus Lucien, the by-product of a long term relationship with model Helen Christensen.

Reedus' forthrightness to the press has been essential to filling out his character. He is literally

Marc Shapiro

fearless in letting the public know just what makes him tick and that, deep down inside, he can't, psychologically, stay in one place too long, as he confessed during an interview with *Elle*. "I'm constantly running away from everything. I'm running away from things on a daily basis.

But ultimately, when the psychological dust settles, Norman Reedus is a creature of his own thoughts, dreams, and ambitions. He's always seemingly looking around the corner for the next opportunity to creatively express himself and has been more than willing to say yes to just about any opportunity, and under any circumstance that crosses his path. And it is this notorious streak of spontaneity which, during his four month hospital stay in Berlin following the accident in 2005, resulted in some very unexpected yet typically Norman-like behavior.

Well into his four month hospital stay in Berlin, Norman was suffering a bad case of cabin fever. He could only go over so many imaginative storylines in his head and carry on so many conversations with his German friend. It was then that he received a ray of mental hope in the form of an opportunity to appear in a short film being prepped in Los Angeles called *Meet Me in Berlin*.

Under the auspices of *Beo Laver Films* in Copenhagen Denmark, *Meet Me in Berlin* was essentially Norman's story. His character has been severely injured in an auto accident and is ravaged by guilt over the fact that he stood up a meeting with a girl. The irony of it all being that, as Norman's character tries in vain to contact her, she, likewise, has been in an accident and is feeling guilt over having stood up Norman's character. Norman readily agreed to do the film and, as he recalled in an interview with *Dixon's Vixens.com*, took the bull by the horns.

"I ended up sneaking out of the hospital and flying to Los Angeles in the middle of the night. I ended up filming with a black and blue face and a patch over one eye."

Even the most jaded pundits have had to admit that a force of attitude and will like Norman has does not come along every day. And for better or worse, he has left a deep impression.

The Walking Dead Executive Producer Gayle Ann Hurd recalled in a *Nylon* interview that "Norman isn't easy to get to know. He doesn't trust easily. He is so damaged deep down. He has a brusque or silent interior."

Playwright Neil Landau, who scripted Norman's first acting role in the play *Maps for Drowners*, told the author in a 2015 interview that "I know this is going to sound bad and I want to emphasize that I didn't really know him at the time. He didn't seem to bathe a lot. He was kind of grungy. He almost looked like he could have been homeless. Who knows, he might have been."

Well known motorcycle designer Carl Lagaspi told the author in 2015 that he had hired Norman after making his acquaintance at an AA meeting. He recalled that personally and professionally the year he spent working for Carl was a combustible one. "He was a little bit mechanical. He could definitely find you a 9/16's wrench if you needed one. He had issues and, at the time, he wasn't getting it. He wasn't dealing with his program real well. Today he's got his shit going on."

To the degree that, in Daryl Dixon, he has stumbled into the role that perfectly accentuates Norman, flaws and all. And it is to his credit that viewers and media observers are hard-pressed to figure out where Norman stops and Daryl begins. Norman is not two stepping the role. He's dirty, often dirtier than his co-stars or seemingly what a scene requires. Norman does sullen, introverted and charismatically distrustful much more than even a typical script requires. And when it comes to killing off *The Walking Dead*, there's nothing stylistic or Hollywood about it. Be it with the bolt of a crossbow or a raw knife thrust into a zombie skull, more than one person has publically speculated that the actor, at the moment the fatal blow is delivered, is dredging up a familiar face from his past and mentally transposing it on an undead just before delivering his kill shot.

And because Norman is seemingly always full bore on the show, it is not too surprising that he's been injured more times than set regulars can count. Norman is quick to acknowledge in a *Rolling Stone* interview that the set medics and the local ambulance service are on a first name basis. "I've been to the doctor so many times."

He went on to acknowledge, in an anecdote reported by *Rolling Stone*, *The Guardian,* and other outlets, a bloody day or real and fake gore. A scene in which Daryl was already covered head to toe with special effects blood was interrupted when a misstep on set resulted in a gash on Norman's head and a torrent of real blood flowing down Norman's face mixing gruesomely with the fake blood.

An ambulance was called and the actor was

whisked off to a nearby hospital where his head was stitched shut. But not before he literally gave an emergency room full of doctors, nurses and patients a heart attack. "The ambulance came and took me to the hospital," he said during a conversation on the television show *The View*. "I come in and they see me just covered in blood and they just start freaking out."

Norman was driven back to the set but it was a given that this day of zombie fighting was over. He was placed in a van and was driven away from the set and to his home. The van eased up a hill and...

"There was an 18 wheeler on its side in a ditch," recalled Norman. "Telephone poles were knocked over. There was a lady on the road screaming that the driver had just had a heart attack and that he was trapped behind the wheel."

In a scene akin to Norman's typical *Walking Dead* heroics, the actor jumped out of the moving van, climbed up the overturned truck to the cab, pulled the driver out and laid him on the ground. "I stood over him, talked to him, telling him, 'Stay with me man! Can you hear me?'"

As fate would have it, the same ambulance that had been called to the set for Norman a few hours earlier had been summoned to this accident and was rounding the corner. The same EMT who had attended to Norman's needs jumped out of the ambulance and made his way toward the accident scene. He was greeted by the sight of Norman, still dressed in blood-soaked clothing and with a bandage covering his stitches, kneeling over the truck driver. Needless to say, the air was thick with adrenaline.

The EMT took one look at Norman and yelled,

"Didn't I just take you to the hospital?" Norman looked up at the EMT, his body flying on the strength of pain medication and adrenaline could only muster a...

"...No it's not me! It's him."

CHAPTER ONE
MOM'S A BUNNY...DAD'S ALL BUSINESS

Norman has spent the last 15 years of his life trying to figure out his family tree. And as he explained in a conversation with *WENN*, he is not there yet. "I have a lot of unanswered questions. I left home at any early age. I travelled around a lot and I was not really close to my father for a lot of years. But now that I have a son, I'm trying to know things and to pass them on."

What finally turned Norman from on the road to discovering his roots was that he finally made peace with his estranged father and was, consequently, told a lot of stories that led him on the path of learning more. With the aid of his younger sister, Leslie, the roots of the Reedus family tree began to show themselves, and often at unexpected moments.

While in Hawaii, filming the *Hawaii 5-0* television pilot, he discovered that his grandfather had once been married to an island girl. It was also around that time that Norman received a missive from the other side of the world, from a relative he didn't know he had. "I recently had a relation of mine contact me from Afghanistan," he told *WENN*. "It turned out he was a Black Ops helicopter pilot, a real bad ass. We got together at one point and he told me some more stories. I was learning a lot of this weird stuff about myself."

For the layman, Norman's backstory is a literal United Nations, encompassing generations of English, Irish, Scottish and Italian offshoots of the Reedus family tree dating back to the early 1700's. The actor's lineage is scattershot with names like Issac Newton Reedus, James David Reedus, Robert Verdell Yarber, Beulah V. Badgett, Bessie Marie Carroll and countless others who were conspicuous by their myriad lifestyles, occupations and status. Along the way the Reedus' and Yarber's met and this is where Norman enters the picture.

Like much of the information surrounding Norman's parents, there is inconsistency in piecing their backstories together. And much of that has depended on alternately how vague or upfront Norman has chosen to be when talking to the press. He has been largely the former when it has come to talking about his father.

What is known is that Ira Norman Reedus was in and out of his son's life for long periods while he was growing up. Norman in later years would usually describe his father as a business man who seemed to move around from job to job with regularity. He would recall in a conversation with *The Sydney Morning Herald* that his father travelled a lot when Norman was young and, among other occupations, often laid claim to the title of motivational speaker.

In an in depth interview with *GQ*, he would be a bit more forthcoming. "He went through several different business. He worked for a printing company for a while and he worked for *TV Guide* for a while."

Personally, Ira Norman Reedus would be a blank slate to his son, with nary a hint forthcoming until he was well into adulthood.

It would be a different story when it came to his mother Marianne Yarber. Norman ran the gamut in acknowledging little or nothing to being effusive in his admiration for his mother. In his eyes, Marianne was a total free spirit in the classic 60's, do your own thing mold. For a period he would willingly extoll the virtues of Marianne to publications as divergent as *The Sydney Morning Herald*, *Men's Journal*, *GQ* and countless others. But when a four hour plus interview session with a publication which, to this day remains unnamed, turned into a scant few paragraphs of him talking about all the amazing and, yes, different occupations she had held, he largely pulled in his horns in talking about his mother's 'interesting' life.

"She was a strong woman, a free spirit," he acknowledged in various ways in the three above-mentioned interviews. "When mom was going to school, she held multiple jobs. She was a Playboy Bunny. She taught high school in The Bronx, taught kindergarten in Harlem. She sold coffins."

As things would play out in later years, Norman would readily concede that both the positive and negative sides of his personality would be formed largely based on the influences of his parents. And perhaps most importantly in the area of relationships and the opposite sex.

And exhibit A in that case being played out in the apparently valid speculation that Norman's parents were never married. In exploring his early years, the press largely assumed that the Reedus' father and mother had been legally married. But Norman, in several interviews, has often danced around the question, addressing the notion with vague one or two word answers. It would become a debatable issue when Norman, in later years, would seem more comfortable addressing the issue when couched as a 'separation.'

Adding to the mystery is the fact that written records of the day seem to have been at odds as to what the truth was. *Geneology.com* indicates that Marianne was married twice but goes no further in terms of when. *Moose Roots.com* indicates that Marianne was only married once, to a David Waples in 1983. Subsequent research ultimately indicated an even split but all were conspicuous by the fact that while a definite date was indicated in the case of the Waples' marriage, no such particulars can be found in the case of Ira and Marianne.

Extensive research on the subject finally turned up a *Texas Divorce Record Index* listed on *Mocavo.com* in which a divorce decree was listed indicating Norman's parents were officially divorced on May 24, 1977 which would logically indicate that they had been legally married at one point, in a rather clandestine way that would seem to defy specifics.

But the status of Ira and Marianne's relationship would take a distant second place to the fact that, in the early months of 1968, Marianne found herself pregnant. Enter yet another gap in time in which the months magically flew by until January 6, 1969…

When Mark Norman Reedus was born.

The mystery and speculation of the relationship would continue unabated over the next couple of years. What is known is that, not long after the birth of Norman, Marianne was once again pregnant and, in 1970, would again give birth, this time to a baby girl named Leslie. For a very young Norman, the memories would continue to be a blur.

As he would confess to *GQ*, "I have no memory of them (his parents) ever living together."

But on a subconscious level, Norman's father would always be with him. Years later, after a reconciliation between father and son and prior to Ira's passing, he would have the name Norman tattooed across his heart. Like everything else connected with his family tree, the actor was initially reluctant to go into any details about the tattoo. But eventually, in a 2013 *Entertainment Weekly* interview, he would feel comfortable enough talking about the ink and that's when people were first clued in to how the wounds went deep.

"With my dad, there were a lot of things I didn't know and a lot of questions I would have liked to have asked him. I would have liked to have known him better."

CHAPTER TWO
TRAVELING SHOES

Hollywood, Florida? Norman did not have a clue.

"I was just a baby," he reflected in *Hobo Magazine*. "We moved from Florida when I was very young. I don't remember anything."

As it would turn out, the very open and, typical of the times, amicable relationship between Norman's parents would allow some interaction between father and son. Ira would pop in and out of the families' life somewhat regularly, if only for brief visits. Norman recalled a fairly platonic relationship during those visits in which the interaction was essentially as a buddy rather than a parent. With little actual guidance in the offing, it was inevitable that young Norman would become a momma's boy.

But with Marianne at the parental helm, it would be in the best possible way.

From a very young age, Norman saw his mother in a near worshipful way, as "quite a unique woman" whose hippie/free spirit attitudes were much in play with his sister's and his earliest memories of her charity work and the ease with which she made them comfortable in what would become a nomadic lifestyle that saw the family leave Hollywood, Florida and live for a time in Northern California, Texas and Oklahoma.

The family moving from town to town quickly became a matter of fact facet of Norman's psyche. In later years he would never overplay the notion that the families' itinerant nature was any big deal. He would quickly dismiss the significance of it all in an interview with *Hobo Magazine* when he said, "I just bounced around a lot."

"My mom was a free-thinking woman and she pushed those free-thinking attitudes onto us," Norman told *The Sydney Morning Herald.* "I don't think I ever thought the whole world revolved around me. I never threw a tantrum."

But along the way, Norman, even as a young child, was seemingly heading down some pretty dark corridors. As soon as his mother would allow, Norman became hooked on horror films, first the classic Universal monsters that populated odd-hour television in the early 70's that he considered cool and, later, when some equally free-thinking family friends took Norman to a drive-in to see the very 'out there' film *The Cars That Eat People*. It was an experience that he offered in a *Complex* interview that turned him irretrievably to the dark side.

"It was crazy," he said. "It was about these people who drive these weird cars with spikes and things coming out of them and terrorize a town full of people. I remember watching that movie and thinking, 'I love this!' There were certain scenes that just stuck in my head."

But easily the movie that struck the deepest chord in Norman's developing psyche was *The Omen*.

Seeing that movie seemingly countless times at an extremely young age pushed the already darkly impressionable Norman to extremes. He became immersed in the character of Damian, the spawn of the devil, and used the occasion of his second grade school year to put his obsession to good use at the expense of his old, shaky, and easily frightened teacher.

"I used to have a second grade teacher who was very old and shaky and nervous," he related in a conversation with television talk show host Conan O'Brian. "So I decided that every day I would go into class and just sit and stare at her like Damian did in *The Omen* just before something terrible happened. It really scared her. It got so bad that when she would go around the class asking us to raise our hands if we had the answer to a question that she would just skip over me and never call on me. Finally at the end of the school year she came up to me and asked why I hated her. I told her I didn't hate her. But I definitely loved what I was doing to her."

Not surprisingly, Marianne was quite tolerant of young Norman's antics. And as any hippie leaning mother of the day would, she both encouraged and contributed to her son's esoteric leanings. Norman was introduced to the idea of live music when his mother took him to a Laurie Anderson concert. And wherever they lived, Marianne made sure there was all kinds of music playing all the time, with a favorite sing-along pastime being mother and son renditions of The Clash's 'Straight To Hell' when they would do dishes together.

"I never had a sheltered life where I did what

everybody else did or did what I was told was the cool thing to do," he explained to *Geocities.com*

Norman soaked up every life experience like the proverbial sponge and formed some early attitudes based on his mother's willingness to let him see some alternative sides of life. He recalled one such lesson in conversation with *Esquire*. "I used to hang out with a bunch of old punk rockers when I was a little kid. I remember going to clubs that I was much too young to be going to. But I learned from being around old punk rockers what it was like to be tough and defiant."

But Norman was not a completely wild child. There were times when he succumbed to normal childhood fantasies. His first celebrity crushes were actress Suzanne Sommers circa the television show *Three's Company* and pop singer Annabella of the pop group *Bow Wow Wow*. Like most children, Norman developed an athletic side. He acknowledged in an *Esquire* interview that he played some baseball and apparently was the team pitcher for a time. Photographic evidence exists that also shows that the very young Norman also played a bit of football and, for a time, was into martial arts. And when it came to career choices, Norman, barely into grade school, had a plate full of ambition, as he explained in *LadyGunn* Magazine.

"I wanted to be a marine biologist. I would watch shows about Jacques Cousteau. He seemed to have the best life so I wanted to be him."

"I wanted to be an astronaut," he recalled in *Geocities.com*. "But I wore contact lenses, was flatfooted and was not that smart,"

However Norman's early childhood years were

9

far from perfect. With his mother's propensity for pulling up stakes and relocating, Norman was faced with constantly being the new kid in school, being in a new area and constantly bouncing around. It was not an enviable situation and Norman was constantly faced with being the outsider trying to fit in and make friends. The actor would acknowledge in later years that being socially awkward did not help, but that through trial and error, he eventually developed a defense mechanism that seemed to ease the process. Quite simply, when he began a new school, he would immediately make friends with the biggest, meanest kid in the school which, effectively, insulated him from being picked on. When he finally made friends with people he actually liked, he would dump his initial friend.

But while he managed to fit in, even on a barely surface level, the results were not always emotionally fulfilling. His first kiss was a prime example, as Norman would explain to *Geocities.com*. "My first kiss was terrifying. I was at a roller rink and I was pushed to kiss this girl in front of these other girls. They set it up and this girl was waiting with puckered lips. They pushed me over to her. I was terrified and it was quick and I was insulted for not making it long and passionate."

Usually Norman's grand plan for fitting in would be derailed when Norman's mother's wanderlust would kick in and she had decided it was time to move and Norman and his sister would be off to greener pastures. With increasing frequency, the destination was on the other side of the world. Marianne's pursuits would typically find the family in such countries as

Spain, Japan, Thailand and Bali. By the time he turned ten, Norman would have his mother's contrary approach to going global down to a science.

"The first trip when I was ten we went to Bonaire, which was off the coast of Venezuela," Norman recounted to *The Sydney Morning Herald*. "We spent a lot of time with the local people and not in hotels. With my mother it was always about getting out and meeting people and hearing their stories...

"...I had a full passport when I was a child."

CHAPTER THREE
GNARLY

By the time Norman reached his early teen years, the mixture of constant moving and exposure to lifestyles well beyond his years had begun to take their toll on any notion of a formal education.

Norman has never been shy about assessing his attitude toward his school history, offering up this succinct tidbit during an interview with *Men's Journal*. "I was a shitty student who used to like to hang out with punk rockers."

However hanging with fellow outcasts did provide the young Norman with a goof or two as he and some friends formed a punk rock band called *Vicious Pricks*. Whether *Vicious Pricks* actually went public to any degree or was simply a garage band exercise has never been revealed. In fact *Vicious Pricks* was apparently a deep, dark secret until Norman started getting famous and journalists started digging. Norman, in a conversation with *GQ*, seemed mildly embarrassed when his rock and roll experiment had been discovered.

"Yes, we had a band in school and we were awful," he chuckled. "It was us singing a few *Black*

Flag songs over and over. I sang but I had no musical talent."

By the time Norman reached the age of 13, he had suddenly found something that he was good at. Tennis.

The very young Norman had developed a strong dexterity for tennis and had proven a better than average player at school sponsored tournaments. It was at one such tournament that Norman was approached by a coach with an offer. "A coach approached me at a tournament and offered to train me because he thought I had potential," Norman recalled in a *Nylon* interview. "He came to my house, spoke to my mom and that was that. I was off."

The Junior Tennis Tour was considered the next step up for aspiring young professionals. Top professional Andre Agassi got his start on the Junior Tour which played a series of tournaments on clay courts throughout the Midwest and North East while training with established coaches. But Norman was not looking beyond the fact that he would be on his own and away from home for the first time in his life. The Junior Tennis Tour had all the trappings of a pro level organization. Kids and coaches stayed in hotels and sponsors supplied players with tennis shoes and equipment. It was on that subject that Norman's memory seems to have wavered. In a *GQ* interview, Norman related that he was supplied with topflight equipment and clothing and shoes while in *Nylon* he proudly boasted of playing in "old basketball shoes and using a toy racquet."

How good Norman was on the tour remained a question mark with only Norman's loose grip on reality to go by. In a *GQ* conversation, Norman said of his tennis prowess, "I was never really that good and I was never really that driven." When talking to *Nylon*, Norman had a different story. "I was good man. But I was surprised that I made it as far as I did."

In fact the consensus was that, based on observers of Norman's tennis skills, the youngster did, indeed, have the potential to take his game to the next level. But something happened at a tournament that would change all that.

"I was at a tournament and I sprained my ankle real bad," he told *GQ*. "I had it injected with something to numb the pain and then I had to soak it in a bucket of ice. All of a sudden I thought 'This isn't fun for me.' I just walked away."…

…And back to a home life that had suddenly become anything but normal. Reportedly Marianne had had boyfriends while Norman was growing up but had been discreet in her relationships so as to not confuse her children. For his part, Norman seemed unaffected by different men coming in and out of his mother's and his lives. But all this had changed when, about the time Norman had gone on his tennis adventure, Marianne had met and, in 1983, subsequently married Douglas Waples.

And just who is Douglas Waples and how did he and Marianne get together? Of the former, Waples is a complete blank slate and while there is a *Geneology on Line.com* reproduction of a Texas marriage certificate that represented the 1983 marriage and a subsequent entry indicated that Marianne would have two more children with Waples in 1987 and 1988. But the complete lack of anything beyond a handful of notations did, in many ways, parallel the sense of emotional and psychological distance between Norman and his biological father.

Some clues, and rather dark ones at that, would occasionally pop up. That Norman once described himself as "a dorky punk rock kid" in *Rolling Stone* went on to hint at Norman as prone to getting into fights. During that self-same interview, Norman matter-of-factly dropped a bombshell that he had been physically abused as a young child.

"I remember being punched and physically abused at home and starting fights with much bigger kids at school to hide what really happened to my face." When pressed by the *Rolling Stone* interviewer as to who abused him, Norman was quick to point out that it had not been his mother or any blood relative. But the *Rolling Stone* interrogator persisted, suggesting that it might have been a boyfriend or his mother's second husband (Douglas Waples) who had abused him. Norman, by this time, having turned evasive on the subject, could only muster a "just different people."

This would be the only time the issue would be addressed and, surprisingly, (given the tabloid nature of the celebrity press) the question of abuse in Norman's life has never again been broached. But a persistent press would occasionally step close to the line of all things personal and Norman would often take the extremely high and patient road in letting prying eyes know that it was none of their business. A candid interview with *GQ* was one of those that seemingly touched a little too close to home and had Norman acknowledging that while bad things had happened to him, he felt it would be dishonorable of him to talk about them.

He elaborated by saying, "There are definitely certain things in my childhood that were pretty gnarly and I don't want to tell you every dirty detail in my life. I don't have any desire to spill my horrible secrets."

But the issue of his questionable upbringing would, in fact, rear its ugly head on occasion. One glaring case being in an interview with *Fan Girl Radio*, a fan-friendly softball throwing offshoot of *The Walking Dead* universe as a spot on question about comparing Daryl to Norman. Norman's response was dead on in exploring his less than ideal upbringing.

"I was a little kid with a smart mouth," he said. "I didn't have the greatest upbringing in certain ways. There were times when I was in danger and I would have to hide from that danger. I'd have to smile when I wasn't supposed to smile."

What was certain as Norman matriculated into high school was that his disillusionment with seemingly everything in his world was palpable. The sense of isolation he must have felt with his mother more occupied with her new family and his half siblings was most certainly pushing him further to the dark side. He was literally sleepwalking through his classes and his days with disinterest and the specter of looking inward following him around like a black cloud. It was obvious that Norman was in an emotional hell.

And for his geometry teacher in particular, it was clear that the young teen needed something to turn him on a more hopeful path. And it would not be formal education. Norman got on well enough with this particular teacher to one day confide in her about his frustrations and unhappiness as he recounted in *Men's Journal*.

"I remember telling one of my teachers that I was going to move to Japan. She was like, 'You should. You should leave.'"

Norman had not expected that kind of response. The more he thought about it, the more appealing the idea of traveling the world like a modern day Kerouac became. His mother, by now up to her eyeballs with married life and two new children, agreed that, despite being fairly close to graduating from high school, being on his own was what her son needed and gave him her blessing.

Once again, Norman would play fast and loose over the years in addressing the issue of the reason why he left home for the open road. But he would admit in an interview with *LadyGunn* that there was much that drove him away. "I left home to do other things. I wasn't exactly running away. It just worked out better for everyone that I left when I did."

Norman dropped out of school in late 1988 and, with very few belongings and very little money, hopped a plane heading for Japan. What is known about his stay in Japan is sketchy at best. What is speculated is that Norman proved a natural when adapting to the bohemian lifestyle and easily blended in with the young and transient population who were traveling the world and, by association, learned the tricks of the trade when living in a land known for extreme opulence.

After a time Norman found his way to London

where he squatted in a house with other fellow travelers, made minimum wage selling postcards in a trendy London shop and subsisting almost completely on a diet of potatoes. Finally Norman was off to Spain where he lived in a tumble down apartment that looked out on the sea. Oh and there was one other thing...

...Along the way Norman met a girl and, for the first time, was in love.

As flirtations and romance played out in the bohemian world, romance was full of spontaneous and impulsive decisions. And so it was not too surprising that, one day, the girl dropped the bombshell that she was tired of Europe and was moving to Los Angeles. Norman was heartbroken and desperate. So much so that shortly after the love of his life hopped a plane headed for Los Angeles, Norman was also on a plane headed to the City of Angeles. Norman was in love...

...And he was not going to give up on love that easily.

CHAPTER FOUR
UNDER A BRIDGE

Norman flew into Los Angeles with pretty much the clothes on his back and not much else. But he most certainly immediately sensed a psychological kinship with the city. He sensed that this was the place where dreams truly became reality. But what he would initially find was that his first love was suddenly on the rocks.

The relationship had not survived the trip to Los Angeles and, shortly after reuniting, the girl broke up with Norman and went back to an ex-boyfriend who, subsequently, whisked her off to Hawaii to get married. Norman was adrift and alone in Los Angeles. Which was fine with him.

"I didn't really know what I wanted," he related to *GQ*. "I didn't really know if I wanted anything."

However his lack of drive or direction was trumped by his natural ability to fit in with like minds. Which led to Norman making his way to a tumbledown section of downtown Los Angeles and an informal group of so called underground artists and street people. This was the stone age of what would become a thriving artist movement in the area and the living conditions were less than ideal if often non-existent. The question has often been speculated upon that Norman was actually homeless much of the time in those early days in Los Angeles and while Norman would never flat out admit to being homeless, he had a descriptive way of dancing around it in a conversation with *LadyGunn*.

"I lived downtown when nobody really lived downtown. It was mostly trash cans of fire under bridges and us."

But with a long history of being adaptable to any situation already behind him, Norman was quick to put the best possible face on what many considered unseemly conditions in a part of Los Angeles that most people would not venture into after dark. As he offered in a look back with *Hobo*, Norman was very much Alice and Downtown Los Angeles was Wonderland.

"It was just so raw and dangerous and on the edge with a cool vibe," he recalled. "Back then there were maybe eight people who lived downtown."

Norman offered that the cool people mixed easily with the homeless who were the areas' primary denizens and who literally brushed shoulders with such pioneering creative personalities as film director Tarsem Singh and would often make for surreal adventures on the streets.

"I remember they had a party downtown for Halloween and there were all these crazy people there," he told *Hobo*. "I remember hearing this old lady on a microphone yelling, 'I see you, you mother fuckers!' I was dressed as a blue horse or something really weird like that. I remember wandering over to where the noise was coming from and, all of a sudden,

Jane's Addiction comes out singing and people were like 'who the hell was that band?' They were amazing. The energy from that band was what LA was like back then."

Norman had evolved into somebody who knew no fear when it came to embracing the unknown and the new. He would acknowledge years later in *Movieline* that his lack of formal training in any of the creative arts was more than offset by a healthy dose of real life when he said, "I'm grateful for life experiences."

Whatever the conditions, Norman used his stay in this primitive arts community to make strides as a fledging artist. His primitive attempts at cutting, sculpting and wielding found pieces of metal and other objects, literally scavenged from trash cans and dumpsters, would prove to be an extension of Norman's long held attitudes, influenced by such artists as Hieronymus Bosch, about the horrific and grotesque also being beautiful. At a very early underground show, Norman reportedly mesmerized viewers with a giant vagina and clitoris cut and shaped out of a piece of rock. Other pieces would combine pieces of metal wielded into madly distorted human and animal visages.

Norman's earliest attempts at getting his art before the public were nothing if not ingenious. Occasionally Norman and his friends would go to the Otis Parsons Art Institute and nail their creations on a wall and get the word out that they were having a show. Norman's ability to make art out of literally anything was typified by a much talked about early effort in which Norman got a series of French doors out of an ad in The Recycler, added an elongated girl's figure and finished the artistic montage off with strands of wire and threw an impromptu party to show it off.

The patchwork quilt that has often been Norman's biography held its secrets fairly well. One of the deepest and darkest being that Norman had become a heavy drinker during his time in Los Angeles and, by 1990 was, allegedly, already a full-blown alcoholic in need of major intervention even before he was barely old enough to drink.

In later years, Norman would gloss over that period, never mentioning any problems with alcohol. But somebody who was there knew different.

It was in the early 90's when Norman met recovering alcoholic Carl Lagaspi at an Alcoholic's Anonymous meeting. Lagaspi, a long-time motorcycle mechanic currently plying his trade in North Carolina, was, at the time, running a motorcycle shop in Venice, Ca. called Dr. Carl's Hog Hospital. In a 2015 conversation with this author, Lagaspi offered that it was Norman and his respective demons that brought them together.

"I'm a recovering alcoholic and that's how I met Norman," he recalled. "He had an alcohol- related issue and that's what brought us together."

Lagaspi had seen his share of alcoholics in his day and could sense that the disheveled and somewhat dirty-looking young man sitting across from him at the AA meeting had the right stuff. "He seemed like he had a heart," remembered Lagaspi. "I can usually tell when people are full of shit and Norman seemed to me to be somebody that wanted to get it."

In the same breath, Lagaspi described the Norman he met that night as being in pretty sad shape. "He had no place to live. He was starving. He had no transportation and he seemed to me to be more or less homeless. He really didn't have anything going on. He needed to make some money and I needed an apprentice type person at the shop."

Norman would start work at Dr. Carl's Hog Hospital the next day. Norman's duties were essentially as a go-for; sweeping up the shop and running for the right equipment when it was asked for. When it was found that Norman had a modicum of mechanical skill, Lagaspi began giving Norman on-the-job training in motorcycle mechanics.

But as was his want, Norman was often dismissive when describing his job in *Movieline* this way. "I was making $7.50 an hour in a motorcycle shop where I mostly shoveled pit bull shit."

As to his attitude while working at the motorcycle shop, Lagaspi, with tongue firmly planted in cheek, said "When he showed up, he did what he was asked to do. I couldn't say he was a jerkoff."

But the mechanic did stop well short of saying that Norman's year long tenure at the shop was a smooth situation. Lagaspi danced around the question of whether Norman would show up for work under the influence or would just not show up at all, preferring to couch an answer in AA jargon.

"I remember we had conversations. I told him, 'Dude, you've got to fly right or I can't have you around here. But he wasn't getting it. It just wasn't his time.'"

Norman's inconsistency in dealing with his drinking issues had been doubly tough on Lagaspi who had developed quite a fondness for the young man. "It made it tough because he stopped doing the right thing in terms of his program. We finally had to have a sit down about it and he wasn't too happy with the ultimatum I gave him. I told him he was going to have to do the right thing and fly right or we were going to have a situation and that he was not going to be happy."

On the occasions when Norman would discuss the final conversation that led to him quitting the job at Dr. Carl's Hog Hospital, the actor presented a radically different version than that of Lagaspi. In his version, Norman explained that he quit after a brewing argument centered around the shop dog, a pit bull, who had been chewing up plastic car parts that had been intended for a project he was working on. Not satisfied with blaming the dog in that initial version, Norman would, years later, tell *E!* that "One day I went to work and one of the guys in the shop was beating one of his dogs. We got into a fight and I just quit."

Whichever side was ultimately true, Lagaspi had mixed feelings about his departure. It was obvious Norman had failed in his attempts to return to sobriety under his tutelage. But it was equally plain that going into the 90's, Norman's boasting that he would be an actor had a ring of truth to the mechanic.

"I knew the crowds he ran in. I knew those people. I hate to say it but he had that look that filmmakers and modeling agencies seemed to be looking for at the time. They were looking for heroin addict types. Everybody in Norman's crowd had dark rings under their eyes and looked like drug addicts…"

"…That's how Norman looked."

CHAPTER FIVE
MAPS FOR DROWNERS

Norman was out of work only a few hours. But it was enough time for the now former mechanic to be well on his way to getting plastered. It was at that moment, predictably not his best, that a friend got a hold of him with the offer to drive up to Malibu for a party being thrown by some rich Hollywood types.

Rich being the operative word for Norman in the worst possible way.

At a very young age, reportedly no more than 17 but possibly into his early 20's when he left the motorcycle shop, Norman had morphed into a defiant, angry young man and much of his impatience and defiance was centered directly on the totems seemingly fostered in Los Angeles. He saw pretentiousness, snobbishness and, although he would never admit it, a certain amount of class envy in Hollywood at every turn. Celebrities, he knew none, and what he perceived as the idle rich who did not have a clue of what humanity was about had also been in his crosshairs. Consequently waving a Hollywood party in front of Norman that night was like waving a red flag in the face of a bull.

Norman recalled in *GQ* that what was most likely going through his head on the way to the party was that "I probably did hate rich people." Also in his mind was the ying and yang of just being fired from his job a few hours earlier and what it all meant to his present and future. One thing Norman would acknowledge years later was that, by the time he arrived at the party, he was already very drunk and about to become disorderly.

Norman was reportedly on the ragged edge from the outset. He masked his discomfort in crowds and social situations by heading straight for the bar. A few drinks down the road and everybody at the party was aware of Norman.

"I became obnoxiously drunk," Norman recalled in *Men's Journal*. "I had a friend's big broken glasses on and was running around the party screaming at people. I was going off. It was a production. Finally I ended up on the second floor screaming at a bunch of Hollywood big wigs and this girl comes up to me and asks me 'Have you ever thought of being an actor?' I was like 'get away from me!' But she persisted and finally I said 'Does it pay?'"

An after party sit down at a local pizzeria called Damianos sealed the deal in a way that only Hollywood could. The woman was, depending on which story you hear, either an agent, a casting director or somebody who had connections (a not uncommon skill in Hollywood) and had agreed to submit Norman for parts even though he was not actually represented by an agent. The process was called 'side –pocketing.' Norman did not care. That he would be paid was what sealed the deal about the time he began to sober up.

Typical of Hollywood, nothing happened overnight and so Norman, essentially, returned to the streets, doing his art and living by his wits. Norman liked the artistic lifestyle and found it the perfect outlet for his long-held bohemian belief system. He was at a crossroads of sorts. He loved the idea of being free to express himself and so thought of art as the perfect life choice. That is until acting suddenly came along.

By 1991, The Tiffany Theater, a landmark of sorts since 1966, had gone from a classic movie house of some renown and a star-studded history to a mecca for independent live theater beginning in the late 80's. But by 1991, the Tiffany was in the home stretch, fighting off progress and a ravenous real estate market with sporadic, independent and often experimental plays in its pair of 99-seat theaters. One of particular note at the time was *Maps for Drowners*.

In a nutshell, *Maps for Drowners* was a comedy about AIDS in which eight people accidentally sublet a New York apartment at the same time and send up society and relationships in a farcical manner, all the while dancing on the edge of a disease that has marginalized society while killing both the body and soul.

Because *Maps for Drowners*, like most small theater productions, had very little money, the show's playwright, Neil Landau, called in a favor as he explained to the author in 2015. "The casting director for the play was Sharon Bioli who was well-known at the time. We were just a little play and we didn't have any money but Sharon did it for me as a favor."

Maura Minsky, co-producer of *Maps for Drowners*, told the author in 2015 that "we did wide casting for all the roles except for Marion Ross and

Lisa Kudrow (her first acting role and way before *Friends*) who were pre-cast. When Norman was sent to us, I was amazed at how super young he looked. He could have been no more than 17 at the time."

For his part, Norman was not too clear of his age at the time except that he was pretty sure he was somewhere in his early 20's. "Oh god!," he told *Imagista*. "All I know is that it was a fucking long time ago."

Playwright Landau recalled that the first time he laid eyes on Norman he was somewhat surprised. "He looked kind of scruffy and rough around the edges. He was not clean cut. He was young and he looked pretty streetwise. He didn't have the typical male model look."

Landau acknowledged that even in the casting process something in Norman seemed to resonate with him. "He was just starting out. He had his photos and I was under the impression that he had just moved here from somewhere. I do remember that even in the casting process, there was something memorable about him. He looked like he had just stumbled out of bed but he immediately gave the impression that he wanted to be taken seriously."

The character Norman was auditioning for was a young surfer boy. He spent most of the play sitting on a sofa and, by all accounts, was a lesser element of the play but, as Minsky recalled, Norman's low key talents were exactly what Landau was looking for. "Basically he had to look a certain way and when Neil wrote the piece he felt that Norman, because of his looks and the way he was able to nonverbally act, completely spoke to the role."

Landau related that, during the casting process, he was caught off balance by Norman's look and demeanor. "He looked like he was drunk or hungover or something. But in reality he was really nice and respectful, kind of quiet and shy. He was quite good in the role except for the fact that he was not quite as funny as the actor we ultimately cast in the role as the lead. But Norman was definitely good and so we cast him as the understudy."

Maps for Drowners opened its six week run at the Tiffany in the summer of 1991.Given the often thankless role of being the understudy in the theater world, the production, as do most others, designated two all-understudy performances during the run of the play. And, as recalled by Landau, Norman made the most of those opportunities. The playwright stated that, on those nights, actors were given the opportunity to invite agents or anybody they wanted to be seen by to the performance.

In a conversation with *Imagista*, Norman conceded to opening night jitters on his first night in the spotlight. "It was terrifying. I had so many lines to memorize. There was a woman in the audience that night named Laura Kennedy who was with William Morris at the time."

"And yes it's true," said Landau, "his very first performance he landed an agent. Everybody was surprised because nobody really knew what to expect from him. And for somebody who had not really been that funny in auditions, when he went on stage during the two understudy performances, he got more laughs than the lead actor. I think it surprised people that he was so good at comedy."

Marc Shapiro

It reportedly also surprised everyone that Norman, given his look and outwardly sullen attitude, was not considered a loose cannon by the other cast members. "I never really got that sense about Norman," said Landau. "He wasn't like a loose cannon or anything like that. He didn't bathe a lot. He looked grungy. He almost looked like he could be homeless. He may well have been. But he was very professional. He always showed up. He was always prepared. He had a strong work ethic."

But while he was the perfect soldier during the run of the play, he would turn to bashing mode years later when discussing the experience with *Geek on Line.com*. "There were a lot of older women in the play and they were kind of stepping on each other's lines a lot. I was like 'this sucks!'"

Maps for Drowners opened to largely mediocre reviews but, through good word of mouth, did good business and was even extended two additional weeks. For Norman, it would be a solid experience. He was barely acknowledged in reviews. But he did manage to get an agent as well a hint of a possible career. But for Norman, the euphoria was ultimately balanced out by a healthy dose of reality.

"Norman was like most actors," reflected producer Minsky. "He did the run of the play and then went looking for his next role. At that point nobody knew that Norman, along with Lisa, would be the one to pop. Years later I heard about *The Walking Dead* and I thought to myself 'I gave that actor his first role.'"

CHAPTER SIX
IF YOU BLINKED YOU MISSED HIM

Following on the heels of his debut in *Maps for Drowners*, Norman had no illusions about being flooded with offers. And when nothing, even with the tacit backing of William Morris, was forthcoming, Norman went back to his bohemian lifestyle. He continued to work at his art and his work would appear sporadically in area shows. He hung out, partied a lot and, along the way had a lot of girlfriends.

Norman would look at that period in his life and point out that, in those early days, he was kind of in a state of flux. He continued to not know what he really wanted and was not intent on either over pursuing or under pursuing anything. Especially women. In an interview with *E!*, he was concise in his shortcomings.

"I can't figure them [women] out," he said. "By no means do I have game."

But he did have instinct and insight when one of many nameless relationships took him down a different road. Around that time a specialty casting agency for music videos had formed by a group of name directors.

"I started dating a girl who was sort of in the

music video world," he recalled to *GQ*. "People like David Fincher, Tarsem Singh and Mark Romaneck. They sort of passed me around to each other. You're cheap, you don't cost them very much money. I'd pay my rent with those."

Norman's video acting career had a rather inauspicious beginning in 1992 when if you blinked you missed him in the *Cat's In The Cradle* video by the heavy rock band *Ugly Kid Joe*. The video's director Matt Mahurin succinctly summed up Norman's contribution in an email to the author when he stated, "Norman only appeared in one brief shot. There is nothing of note to relate."

Norman had a bit more going on in his next music video, Keith Richards' *Wicked as It Seems*, a truly down and dirty, beyond questionable behavior romp. Once again Norman was little more than part of the scenery, a fleeting, black and white image of shirtless and smoking bravado who sums it all up halfway through the video by flashing devil's horns.

What may have been Norman's most bizarre music video turn came in 1994 with Bjork's *Violently Happy*. Known for her surreal antics and for turning preconceived notions on their head, the singer aimed her sights directly on Norman in a brief sequence in which the actor, dressed in pure pop quasi drag and looking alarmingly feminine, is seen taking dangerous looking shears to a very *Duran Duran* style mullet, pouting and posturing as the locks fall and finally writhing around in a padded cell.

Fake Plastic Trees by Radiohead (1995) was a surreal outing outlining the comings and goings of 'out there' characters in a futuristic supermarket. For his part, Norman's cameo appearance, to the tune of three swift cuts, has the actor playing with a toy trolley. Typical of *Radiohead's* droll 90's attitude the reviews of the video were decidedly mixed.

Norman would revert to form in that same year's *Strange Currencies* music video by *REM*. Ultimately the sight of Norman skulking in and out of shadows in a trench coat were very much in the actor's wheelhouse and would resonate fairly deeply in viewer's minds. Because in those scant seconds we saw Norman, in the best possible sense, channeling Norman.

Whatever it was in the novice actor, when it came to music videos, Norman seemed more than capable of projecting a stylistic element of tension and danger that could be shoehorned into just about any music video and, for whatever amount of time he was on screen, people would, quite simply, get it.

This was no more evident than when Norman was cast in *The Goo Goo Dolls* video for their song *Flat Top*. In the sequence in which Norman is seen putting the moves on his girlfriend while they are watching television, the message seemed clear. Rite of passage, youthful passion, etc. But there was suddenly more to it than mere cliché.

In the few moments that Norman was on screen, there was a sense of discomfort and unease. Norman projected a look that said almost anything could happen at any moment…

And most likely would.

CHAPTER SEVEN
DISCOVER ME

But in between music video jobs, there was little going on, professionally, that would indicate that Norman was about to blossom into Hollywood's next big thing. William Morris, banking on his critical achievement in *Maps For Drowners*, did what any talent agency would do, which was to send him out for several auditions after the play ended its run. None of which resulted in a job.

"I did my first movie at 28," he reflected to *Stnrd*. "It was the right time for me. If I was any younger when I got into acting I would have killed myself. I would have been a complete idiot. I would have been a fucking lunatic."

Norman did not take those early rejections well. An impatient sort who was still not sold on acting as a way to make a living, he quickly tired of rejection and decided to return to his true love, art. But while he continued to grow as an artist, with his works appearing in numerous shows to promising notices, reality quickly set in. "But then I was starving," he reflected to *Geocities.com*, "and so I jumped back into acting."

And the endless auditions that produced no work. The closest Norman came to actually landing a role in the early 90's was the film *Gun Crazy*, a 1992, reboot of an early 50's B movie potboiler. Reportedly it was close but no cigar in that film.

The artist in Norman would continue to play an important role in film choices, especially when it came to big studio pictures. Such was the case during one audition in the mid 90's for a big budget, big studio science fiction epic called *Starship Troopers*. The Hollywood scuttlebutt, as reported by *Movieline*, was that Norman had all but landed his first part in a giant bug movie that would, most certainly, debut in thousands of theaters. Commercially it seemed like *Starship Troopers* would be a sure bet to jumpstart Norman's career. But after a quick read of the script, Norman proclaimed to anyone who would listen that "this movie was going to suck." The result was that *Starship Troopers* decided to go in a different direction.

Norman's 'attitude' finally found a kindred spirit in 1997 when he took an audition with the current hot kid on the horror block, director/actor/writer Guillermo Del Toro for a small part in another horror bug epic, *Mimic*, in which mutant cockroaches run amuck in the big city. Norman and Del Toro immediately hit it off. They were both street smart and artistically inclined. It was, according to Norman in *Out Magazine*, an important first step up the Hollywood ladder. "*Mimic* was my first film and my first part. It also allowed me to get my SAG card." As for his breakthrough role, it was definitely not boring. Norman played Jeremy, somebody who does a bit of flexing while looking pensive as a sewer worker and who ultimately gets eaten by a cockroach.

Mimic gave Norman a front row seat as to the logistics of making a big budget, studio film but the experience still left the actor emotionally in the dark as to his true acting abilities. "I really didn't know what the fuck I was doing," he told *Fugue*.

His comment was made shortly after he was unexpectedly plucked from the Hollywood pool to star in a very small but very character driven drama called *Floating*. *Floating*, would do only modest box office on a limited theatrical release in 1999, told the story of a mid-twenties petty criminal whose days and nights revolve around taking care of his wheelchair-bound father. The film was a classically aimed coming-of-age story, fairly low-key and, by degrees, quiet in tone, but nevertheless, for Norman, it was a daunting and, yes, challenging task.

By all accounts, Norman was more than capable of playing low-key while demanding attention with every look, snap of dialogue and a quite natural acting quality. Which, in hindsight was a lot to ask of an actor carrying an entire film for the first time. And for his part, Norman seemed quite up to the task…

…Until a scene near the very end of filming literally brought Norman to an emotional standstill. The scene in question called for the father to struggle out of his wheelchair and give his son a hug. The tension on the set was palpable. To get it right would, creatively, bring down the house. Fifteen minutes before the scene was to be shot, director William Roth went over to Norman and asked him how he wanted to get ready? Norman did not have to dig too deep for inspiration. Norman and his real life father had recently reconnected after some years apart and, as it turned out, his father was also wheelchair-bound because of an illness. Norman asked the director for a cell phone and a few minutes by himself.

Norman rang up his father and they talked for several minutes. As Norman recalled in *Fugue*, the conversation was about nothing in particular before saying goodbye to his father and walking back to the set. The scene was shot in two takes. The first take, although reportedly quite good, had to be scrapped because Norman had visible snot coming out of his nose. The second take, without the snot, also appeared to go quite well. Norman was not really sure how it had gone as the cast and crew were immediately released for lunch. Norman returned to his trailer for a quick nap and was on his way back to the set when one of the grips came over to him.

Norman recalled in *Fugue* that, "He stopped me and said 'I want to tell you something. At lunch nobody ate and nobody spoke. Everybody just sat there quiet.'"

Norman walked away from that conversation, having reached an unexpected turning point. He realized that acting was not all about being a star and making lots of money. It was suddenly about doing good work with good people and making the result something that could get to people in any number of ways. For Norman, he suddenly had the perfect vision of art and commerce.

Word quickly got around that Norman was pretty damned good at crying and, for a time, Norman was being sent out on any audition that would require the actor to shed a tear.

As if exemplifying his new attitude, he went from star to way down the cast list in a small role in the 1998 family saga *I'm Losing You* by director/novelist Bruce Wagner from his novel by the same name. While essentially a small independent film, it had all the trappings of mini/major when it came to getting the film into theaters and would do respectable business upon release and succeeded in getting Norman out in the public.

Norman had pretty much settled into a modus operandi when it came to choosing films. If the role was good and the script was on point, it did not matter if the offer was big studio or independent. He never had to think twice about doing it. Which was essentially the criterion for his agreeing to take on the role of the confused young man Harold in *Six Ways To Sunday*, a tale of crime and his reaction to his overly attentive mother Katie, played by rock star Deborah Harry.

Essentially a standard issue crime drama, *Six Ways to Sunday* made its psychological bones on the back of the relationship between Harold, whose father had long since left, and Katie who is overcompensating by being an overly aggressive and, by degrees, suggestive mother whose intentions, on a subliminal level, soon become obvious. Adding to the insanity of it all is Harold attempting to shake off his demons and become a man by joining the Mafia and killing people in various, graphic vignettes.

Norman recalled in a *The Free Library.com* interview that *Six Ways to Sunday* also occasioned his very first on screen kiss with co-star Deborah Harry. But it was far from an intimate moment.. "Those scenes may look cozy and intimate but there are 200 people around you holding lights and picking their nose, so it's so not sexy when you're doing it."

Norman is quite good as the confused young man and appears to mirror quite effectively the subtle nuances of Norman Bates in *Psycho*. The psychological aspects of his character and the relationship with his mother are the major attraction in this little-seen movie and were of major interest in an interview with *Out*.

"Harold was only half psychotic," explained Norman. "The other half is shy and nervous around girls. The violence was really fun. I liked the part where I sliced my friend's throat. I liked cutting him up. It was nice. I end up grinding his skull with a jackhammer. It was great."

During the conversation with *Out*, Norman addressed his own obsessions in various degrees of candor. He laughingly self-diagnosed himself as being "a neck and feet" guy and, in a slightly more serious vein, confessed to finding the way people talk a big turn-on, going so far as to confess that the girl he was currently dating said 'idear' rather than 'idea' and that was a big turn-on.

What Norman did not know was that the fates were conspiring on the set of *Six Ways to Sunday* to turn his life in a totally unexpected direction. Well-known photographer Ellen Von Unwerth was on the set one day taking some casual snaps of the actors. Norman had been largely low down her pecking order of who to photograph but there was something in Norman's look that jumped out at her. What happened next is the kind of fairytale that Hollywood and journalists looking for an obvious angle thrive on. At this point, it has been told enough times that Norman is even tired of talking about it. But back when he was not well-known, and in such outlets as *The Tonight Show*, *Fugue Magazine* and countless others, it went something like this...

"Yes, I dabbled in modeling. I say dabbled because I'm kind of short and round which is not really the modeling type. Anyway, Ellen Von Unwerth, that big time photographer, knew some people on the film and came by to shoot some publicity stills and took some pictures of me. What I didn't know was that she had a meeting with Muiccia Prada, the creative designer for the Prada fashion line and said, 'you should take a look at this kid' for their upcoming actor-based ad campaign. The next thing I knew I was getting a call from my manager who said 'it's between you and Nicholas Cage for Prada.' I said that's cool but what's Prada? He explained to me what Prada was and that I would get paid a lot of money and get a free trip to Paris. It was a no brainer."

Norman flew to Paris where he joined the other actors in the campaign, William Dafoe, Joaquin Phoenix, Tim Roth and others in a literal star-studded aid campaign that saw the actors posing in Prada's latest clothing line in hip, modern and often surreal settings. Norman was admittedly naïve when it came to the inner workings and attitudes surrounding modeling and so, when not in front of the camera, he reverted to being just Norman which, on one occasion, turned into a hilarious faux pas.

On his very first night of work, Norman was getting ready for a shoot when an assistant gave him a

Prada sweater to wear and a soda to drink. While in an animated conversation with another model, Norman spilled the soda all over himself and the sweater. Without batting an eye, Norman took off the sweater and used the pricy garment to wipe up the soda. Norman had no idea that, in the modeling world, to wipe up a spill with anything from Prada was akin to committing a crime against nature.

For his part, the photos featuring Norman were alternately seductive and defiant set in a world of high fashion/hip society. Norman was tolerant but far from happy with the glamorous assignment as he would acknowledge in a *Content Mode* interview.

"I'm not happiest when I'm just standing around getting my picture taken. I'm really not that comfortable."

That statement showed that Norman could be diplomatic and even-handed even when he was talking about something he did not care for. But by the time *GQ* got around to probing his modeling days, Norman was showing his rebellious side when he said, "I hated it. I fucking hated it."

But he came to realize how important such an opportunity could be in 1997 when a massive ad campaign for Prada, with many of the ads featuring Norman, hit the magazine pages, billboards and the sides of buses, seemingly covering every blank space on the planet.

Norman Reedus, in the vernacular of Hollywood, was now on everybody's lips. It was serious business but Norman, as a good-humored guest on *The Tonight Show*, could only see the humor in the notoriety. "My five friends and I shared the same suit for a year. After I did that shoot, we suddenly all had suits."

41

Typical of Norman, the actor pretty much ignored much of the notoriety and went about his business as only Norman could. It is not known for certain to what degree big budget, big studio offers began to come Norman's way in the wake of the Prada unveiling. What is known is that Norman would continue to fill out his acting card with a trio of small studio and/or independent films that, admittedly, few people would ever see. *Reach The Rock*, *Dark Harbor* (another daring bit of business in which Norman played a gay lover who has an on-screen kiss with actor Alan Rickman) and *Davis Is Dead* flashed by in a blur with little or no press or recognition. But as it would turn out, *Vanity Fair* was, indeed, paying attention to Norman.

To the surprise of many, the high-profile magazine made Norman a last minute addition to its 1999 Rising Talent To Watch issue. Traditionally, that annual issue would serve as a calling card to producers, directors and casting agents that these were the news kids on the block that they should consider. The actor would often joke that the other actors who made the *Vanity Fair* list might be looking down their noses at this seeming unknown catching the brass ring. But quick with the positive spin, he simply said there were more than enough jobs in Hollywood to go around.

Norman should have been elated, but by 1999 he had more pressing matters to deal with.

Norman was in love and he was about to become a father.

CHAPTER EIGHT
SHY BOY MEETS WONDER WOMAN

By 1997 Norman was seemingly rounding into shape when it came to his love life. The many creative worlds he had travelled in offered an endless array of dating opportunities. Norman was still shy and tentative around the opposite sex but he was not a monk. He definitely had an eye for beauty which was why models seemed to top his dating habits.

"I'd been with several models," he acknowledged in *GQ*, "but none of it was serious."

By the time his Prada ads began their run in the fashion world, Norman was both beginning and ending one of those non-serious cycles with *Sports Illustrated* swimsuit model Bridget Hall. Norman, who was pushing 30 at the time, may well have felt the need for a more serious relationship.

Enter Helena Christensen.

Helena Christensen was a Danish model, photographer, clothing designer, and a hippie at heart. She came into prominence in the 1980's when the phrase 'super model' had not yet come into vogue. She was the face and body that graced billboards and magazine covers for nearly a decade. And when the grind of it all became a grind and 'burn out' was looming on the horizon, she walked away to try her hand at photography, surfacing occasionally for the odd modeling gig but always with an eye on what the world would next offer to challenge her.

One did not have to look too deep to see a kindred spirit to Norman in the making. But it would be a challenging matchup. Helena was already well-established while Norman was still scrapping in the trenches to find himself. Norman would later acknowledge in a conversation with *EA Destination.com* that he knew the reality of their standing in the world when he said, "Helena is famous and she was more famous than me when I met her."

And how the pair met, filtered through the memories and perceptions, had all the makings of an old-fashioned romance done up as hip melodrama. Helena, according to *The Daily Mail*, had recently returned from Australia where she had attended the funeral of former longtime lover, *INXS* lead singer Michael Hutchence and was feeling blue in the aftermath. While hanging out with her friend, photographer Yelena Yemchuk, Norman came up in conversation.

"Helena saw a picture of me that Yelena had taken and said, 'who's that?," Norman related in a *New York Post* interview. "Yelena said, 'oh that's fucking Norman.'"

Helena seemed interested and Yelena seized the opportunity to get her friend out of her funk by talking up Norman and suggesting that the two might meet. As it turned out, a mutual friend of Yelena and Norman's was having a birthday party and, although reluctant at first, Helena agreed to go along with her friend for some drinks and, perhaps, a chance to meet this interesting-looking actor.

As it turned out, Norman was being, likewise, set up by his friends and had agreed, with equal trepidation, to go to a Japanese restaurant where the party was being held. He recalled in *Nylon* that the buildup initially succeeded in pointing out his admitted cowardice. "Some mutual friends of ours were like, 'You should meet this girl. You would love this girl. You guys would hit it off.' When she came into the restaurant I didn't want to look at her because I knew that if we started up a conversation, it would be serious from that point on. I was just cowardly."

Eventually glances and sly smiles across the crowded restaurant turned into casual conversation. And despite any nervousness, their attraction was mutual and instantaneous. "She's a real cool gal," Norman acknowledged of his early impressions of Helena to *The New York Post*. "She's really smart and we laugh at the same crap." With nary a hint of embarrassment, Helena jokingly related in interviews with *The Daily Mail* and *The Observer* that she was all over Norman the entire evening and was "snogging his face off."

Almost immediately Norman and Helena were a committed couple. But knowing how ravenous the tabloid press and paparazzi could be at the hint of a celebrity relationship, they would not publically announce that they were together for nearly two years. However they would prove fairly carefree in being seen together as they hopscotched back and forth between Europe and the United States, doing a deft juggling act between professional and social obligations while cultivating their personal relationship. The couple formally went public when they were photographed together at the 1998 MTV Movie Awards. Helena always seemed quite comfortable in any social situation and easily fit in Norman's world. On the other hand, it was on the job training for Norman when it came to their differences in status in the eyes of the celebrity world.

"Being with Helena, it was always beautiful and daunting," Norman revealed to *Vanity Fair Italia.* "When we walked into a room everybody turned [to look at us)]. Someone almost choked on their food once. For me, it was like I knew nothing of that world. It was like taking a crash course. In her place I would not have endured all that attention."

That the relationship was working so well in the first year was often a mystery to even the couple's most ardent supporters. In a candid conversation with *The Observer*, Helena, in bemused tones, revealed the nuts and bolts of how they got along and, in the process, added a few insights into Norman's character. "Norman and I are the same. We're both Capricorns and we both have Scorpio rising. We've been told that's the worst possible combination. We're both stubborn as mules and we argue for hours. It's volatile but it keeps us on our toes."

When two free thinkers get together, anything can happen and usually at a lightning fast pace. Such was the case when Norman and Helena took the opportunity to announce that they were officially a couple to, matter of factly, also let the world know that Helena was pregnant.

The cynics in the pop culture blogosphere turned up their tabloid noses at the notion that yet another budding power couple was making their 'oops' moment public. Norman got wind of those reports and reverted to a chivalrous tone to defend his ladies' honor. "We're not legally married but we're definitely together," he told *Norman Reedus posterous.com*. "Helena and I decided to have a baby right from the start. We both just knew it was right. Sure we were nervous about having a baby because we knew it would be a huge responsibility."

But once he got through waxing adult on the situation, leave it to Norman to humorously understate the blessed event.

"Helena and I were pretty serious," he told *GQ* with tongue firmly planted in cheek. "I guess this means we were pretty fucking serious."

In their own way, Norman and Helena were ecstatic at the prospect of being parents. In the early months of the pregnancy both were working and traveling which was the way it had always been. But there appeared to be a heightened sense of awareness to the notion of each having their first child. Norman was reportedly quite attentive and always made time to be with the mother of his child.

"In the end, she's the woman I'm going to spend the rest of my life with," he told *Nylon*. "Whatever she does, I'm going to support it."

Likewise, Helena, who had always been known for her independence, was now, reportedly, pulling in and presenting a nesting frame of mind.

Helena, went into labor in October 1999 at the Denmark National Hospital in Copenhagen. According to an interview with Helena in *NW Magazine*, it was a strenuous moment with Helena constantly begging for painkillers but bravely toughing it out and, on October 13, 1999, Mingus Lucien Reedus was brought kicking and screaming into the world. At the time of his son's birth, Norman was in Mexico working on a film called *Beat*. Helena, reveling in the moment, told *NW Magazine* that she was deliriously happy, wanted to have another child in the not too distant future and that the couple were already making plans to be married the following year.

Norman was quite content to let Helena do the talking. Because while he tended to hide things well, he was the Norman equivalent of over the moon when he talked to *Nylon*. "We're very excited. We couldn't be happier. Everything is really nice right now."

CHAPTER NINE
NORMAN KILLS

Norman was caught in a not too uncommon reality in Hollywood by the time he met Helena for the first time in 1998. He had done quite a few films and, along the grapevine, had given what many considered solid performances. But owing to the vagueness of distribution and studio deals, just about everything Norman had done to date had either not yet been released or released in such a limited number of theaters for such a short run that few, if any, had seen them. Reportedly the actor could point to as many as five films that were still in limbo. A minor blip of recognition did surface in 1999 when *Floating* received a very marginal release that caught the eye of the New England Film and Video Festival which saw fit to award the actor with a Special Jury Award for Best Acting Performance.

Still Norman persisted, taking any job that hinted at the kind of edginess he craved, no matter how big, or as it often was in the actor's case, how small the part. Norman found the right kind of role in the direct to DVD retelling of Shakespeare's Hamlet in the Stacy Title directed *Let the Devil Wear Black*, a film that slipped through the cracks on a wave of good reviews and praise for the ensemble cast of actors. Norman had little to do in the big studio film *8MM* as he was well down the cast list of star Nicholas Cage. But again it was the sheer, psychological horror of the overall piece that carried the day over a less than meaty part.

Norman loved the idea of working in a creative world and would seemingly take any reasonable job that came his way. But he was psychologically reaching a crossroads. He was still emotionally attached to the art world and putting in a lot of time, alone and in collaboration with other artists, in getting his name out there. His work was being seen in galleries which fueled his desire. His relationship with Helena was blossoming. While acting was still very much an attraction, the frustration of the process often had Norman contemplating a change of career.

That was until he crossed paths with a bloody killing spree of a movie called *The Boondock Saints*.

The Boondock Saints, written and directed by bartender/bouncer turned filmmaker Troy Duffy, tells the story of two fraternal twins, Connor and Murphy MacManus, who become vigilantes after killing two members of the Russian Mafia in self-defense. Their mission? To get rid of all crime and evil in the city of Boston by whatever means necessary. Which entailed much gunfire, blood and ultra-violence.

The film's script had become an immediate hot property. But as often happens to hot properties in Hollywood, over a two-year period beginning in 1997, the script had been through several studios, several producers and was going through casting disagreements and budget problems about the time a copy of *The Boondock Saints' script* fell into the Norman's hands.

"I remember the script going around when I was living in LA," he said in an *Icon Vs Icon* interview. "I read it and thought it was amazing. I went out and met Troy [Duffy] at a bar and we started talking about the storyline and the part. I really wanted to do it."

As did just about every big name actor in Hollywood. Names like Sylvester Stallone, Mark Wahlberg and Ewan Macgregor were being tossed around daily. And on a pure name recognition level, Norman knew that he was at a distinct disadvantage. "I hadn't really done anything. In a sense it would be my first film," he admitted to *Icon Vs Icon*.

But while he continued to lobby the filmmaker on his own, Norman also took the step of going straight to the top to state his case. At the time, Miramax Films held the option for *The Boondock Saints* and, coincidentally, Norman was also being considered for a part in another film being done by Miramax. Norman was slated to go to New York to take a meeting with Miramax honcho Bob Weinstein to discuss the other project. At the meeting, Weinstein asked Norman if he wanted to do the film. Putting on his big boy attitude, Norman told Weinstein that he would do the first film if he would let him do *The Boondock Saints*. Weinstein would not give him a definite yes or no and so the project remained in limbo while Norman returned to Los Angeles and continued to talk to Troy about him playing the part of Murphy.

More drama ensued. Miramax ultimately backed out of *The Boondock Saints* and independent Franchise Pictures jumped into the fray, albeit at a reduced shooting budget. Big names for the lead roles continued to be speculated on and dismissed before veteran actors Sean Patrick Flannery and Willem Dafoe took two of the three lead roles. In the meantime, Troy had eventually succumbed to Norman's insistence that he could play Murphy and fought tooth and nail with the producers who insisted that a high profile name should have the part. Troy eventually won out and Norman, feeling both excited at the prospect of what he considered a meaty role and nervous at what he felt was the enormity of the project, reported to *The Boondock Saint's* set.

"It was one of my first things," he told *Icon Vs Icon*. "I had no idea. I was just happy to be on a movie set! I was just taking it all in. I was like 'What do I do? How does this all work?' "

It would not take long for Norman to figure it out.

The Boondock Saints was a literal three-ring circus. Troy could be a tempestuous and abrupt and alternately an encouraging and inviting personality. There was a guerrilla style feel to the production that moved at lightning speed through the days and script pages. Dafoe and Flannery were generous in helping Norman through the rough spots and just as quick to make him the butt of jokes. Norman's affinity for the dark side of life would ultimately make his Murphy the ideal vigilante as well as the silent projector of emotion and determination during the more introspective moments.

Norman emerged from *The Boondocks Saints* reenergized as to the power of film to create great art and his place in the movie-making world as a creative medium. It would be some years later when *The Boondock Saints* overcame further obstacles on the road to becoming one of the first internet cult films, that he would discover that he was suddenly famous as well.

When not working, Norman made a beeline back to Helena who was, by this time, well into her pregnancy. These moments were, most likely, as tense as they were loving. Their time apart for professional reasons had been an often un-said facet of their relationship. But with a baby on the way and, by association, Norman's working life seemingly on the upswing, the increasing time apart, must have been tough on emotions and nerves. But ultimately there seemed to be an understanding between the couple that they loved each other and that they would be together when it counted.

From the beginning, Norman had adopted a rather lackadaisical attitude regarding his career. He had only been in his agent's office twice. Fortunately his agent had been quick to size up his client as a certain type and had been equally quick to ship any script with an eye toward the dark and quirky Norman's way. Such was the case when the script for *Beat* came his way. *Beat*, written and directed by Gary Walkow, tells a slice of beatnik history in the events surrounding William Burroughs' killing of his wife Joan Vollmer during a drunken argument. The film, which toplined Kiefer Sutherland and Courtney Love, cast Norman as the chameleon like sidekick Lucien Carr, capable of murder in his own right as well as personal double dealing. For Norman, *Beat* would be a solid and subtle turn in yet another film that would only get a marginal release but proved a solid outing in adding depth to Norman's well-defined and nuanced style of acting.

Norman was in Mexico working on *Beat* when his son was born. It had been one of those realities Helena and Norman had agreed was alright. But beneath the

53

surface there most likely was disappointment for both of them. However Norman would salve his disappointment by winning a bet with Helena that, if the child were a boy, he could pick the name. As it turned out jazz buff Norman was a big fan of the legendary Charlie Mingus... Mingus it would be.

Helena and Norman had paid their due diligence during the pregnancy. When they were together they would discuss at length how the logistics of being parents, in Norman's case often from a distance, would play out. But Norman was the first to say in an interview with *The Free Library.com* that the moment Mingus was born, his attitude toward parenting and his life irrevocably changed.

"I suppose the biggest change you make is how much time and devotion you take from yourself and put in other areas," he said. "Before I had Mingus, I pretty much made all my decisions around myself. Now I have to schedule everything around his nap and dinner time."

With their family now including a newborn and Helena adopting the position of stay-at-home mother, Norman, perhaps feeling further pangs of responsibility, seemingly jumped into an endless string of movie roles. In *Deuces Wild* he essayed the prototypical 50's scumbag, Marco Vendetti, an up and coming drug dealer who makes his bones by killing the brother of the film's hero. At that point his old *Mimic* friend Guillermo Del Toro rang Norman up with the offer to play an action packed comic book type of role in *Blade 2*, opposite Wesley Snipes and Kris Kristofferson.

The role of Scud, a criminally inclined weapons'

expert and the assistant to the half-man/half-vampire hero, was a sign that Norman's profile was definitely on the upswing. It was a fairly substantial part in a sequel to a commercially successful film from a big studio. But for Norman it boiled down to a fun ride being directed by a friend. It was also an introduction into how logistically challenging big summer popcorn movies can be.

Norman was more than willing to do his own stunts but even he must have had second thoughts when one trick required him to leap from a ceiling 40 feet above the ground and do a backflip in mid-air. There is also a scene (spoiler alert) where Scud meets his demise after being mauled by two vampires and ends up exploding. For that bit of business, he had to endure the process of a full body cast so several life-sized puppets could be made.

But easily the highlight of the Prague-lensed *Blade 2* was that Helena and Mingus came over for a visit. Mingus was just beginning to walk and did not take kindly to the rules and regulations of filmmaking as Norman laughingly remembered in *The Free Library.com*. "He was great. He was running around screaming and we'd all be going 'sshh!'"

During this period, Norman also found the time to spread his wings in a couple of well-below the radar opportunities. He started up his own production company in Spain and began working on his company's first project, a zombie western tentatively titled *City of The Dead* with director David Barto, which, owing to the vagaries of the business, has been in production limbo for a number of years and has yet to be made. And in a truly outlandish twist, Norman agreed to go to China to be the only American actor among an entire Chinese and Japanese cast in a very strange bit of cinema called *Great Wall, Great Medicine* in which Norman plays a young man studying eastern medicine who is attempting to get a patent for a colon cancer-friendly toilet.

Well into 2000, Norman continued his juggernaut pace, appearing in a somewhat kinky bit of psychological business in *Gossip*, a comedy thriller entitled *Sand* and a low-budget character study called *The Beatniks*. Only *Gossip* would receive even a marginal theatrical release and while Norman reportedly did solid work, the three films and his participation in them was negligible.

In the meantime, Helena was chaffing at the increasingly long periods that Norman was not around. As Mingus grew older, she was by fits and starts returning to the working world as a photographer and creative director for *Nylon Magazine* which salved her boredom during the hours of being alone.

But the press was beginning to notice that Helena was regularly spotted alone or with toddler Mingus in a kangaroo pack but rarely with Norman. The expected tabloid speculation was that the couple had broken up and that Helena was already seeing somebody else. Norman apparently did not see much point in responding to the stories but, apparently, Helena did.

She would regularly laugh off the charges in outlets like *Contact Music*, *The Daily Mail* and *The Observer*, letting the world know that, in no uncertain terms, there was no trouble in paradise.

"Norman's always around and we're always taking little trips to Sweden and we have time alone," she explained to *The Observer*. "Maybe, in a couple of years, I'll be ready to add to the brood."

Well into 2001, the nature of Norman and Helena's relationship was of major concern to the prying gossip and tabloid press and, if anything, it made the couple less camera shy. Pictures of the couple were regularly on the internet and at such events as London Fashion Week and, perhaps most telling, the couple made a splash of their togetherness when they both came out of their respective modeling hiatuses to appear together in two high profile European ad campaigns.

The first was a splashy get together for Allesandro Dell'Acqua. Some months later, Norman and Helena were back together in front of Terry Richardson's camera lens for an expansive ad campaign for UK clothing giant H&M. The latter was an exercise in humor and subtle sexuality as the photos of Norman and Helena told the product-friendly story of a couple breaking up and making up in 50's Cuba.

If there was any doubt that Norman and Helena's relationship was on the rocks, that shoot laid the rumors to rest. You can't fake the looks that passed between them during the shoot and the ease in which they smiled and joked in between set-ups.

Norman and Helena appeared very much in love.

CHAPTER TEN
DONE AND DONE

But being in love could not keep Norman away from his other passions.

Along the way Norman had developed a truly auteur attitude toward his art and choices, especially when it came to choosing film projects. With the public currency he bought with *The Boondock Saints*, it was a fairly sure bet that Norman was being offered his fair share of parts in big studio, slam dunk commercial projects that, doubtless, would have paid a boatload of money. However, in what seemed, to many, to be a psychological move, Norman seemed to be running the other way.

In short order, the actor had signed on to do a trio of very small, independent projects that would most likely end up going direct to video or a tiny theatrical release. But Norman's ongoing mantra that anything he did had to have a creative/quirky quality to it remained consistent. He would often hint at the advantages of independent films offering a more welcoming and collaborative environment and, without naming names, he claims a couple of films on a larger plane had ultimately not been a joyous experience. Whatever the reasoning, Norman, admittedly, was finding room to creatively move in his latest films.

"I've done so many bad guys I thought it would be nice to play the hero," Norman said during an on set interview that ran on *YouTube* for the first of the aforementioned films *Octane*, a psychological edge-of-the-seat thriller in which Norman played a mysterious anti-hero called The Recovery Man. "It's subtle, real-time stuff. You never know what he's about and what he's about to do."

Tough Luck, another film made during this period, is a classic tale of deceit and double cross when a shady character played by Norman is hired to bump off a man's wife only to discover a world where duplicity and double dealing are the watchword.

Nobody Needs to Know was a surreal mixture of *The Day of The Locust* and a *Shadow* radio serial in which unknowns make their own destiny by taking control in a surreal look at the price one pays to make it in the world. Norman played solid support, lurking on the edges before his fate is sealed by a gunshot.

That Norman could be totally on the fringe when it came to questionable career moves and not bat an eye was exemplified in 2002 when he agreed to take a very small part in a very out there drama/comedy about the hardcore gay lifestyle called *Luster*. Cast with largely gay actors, *Luster* is, as one could imagine, graphic and blatant in a number of scenes, including one in which Norman, going under the name Sex Tool Delivery Boy, makes a delivery to one of the main characters who makes a big play for Norman before turning him over to his boy toy who, in turn,

Marc Shapiro

gets down to the business of giving the delivery boy oral sex.

The entire sequence involving Norman clocks in at about a minute and a half. Did Norman need the gig that badly? Was he doing it for kicks? Did he see it as a form of artistic expression? Only Norman knows for sure and, to this point, he has not spoken publically about *Luster* but his name on the cast list and the appearance in question, is on several websites for anyone to see ,so he obviously is not losing any sleep over it.

Norman had never expressed an interest in guest starring in series television. But there was something in the notion of doing a two-episode shot in *Charmed*, the long running, relatively innovative and largely family-friendly PG rated tale of three young witches. In the role of Paige's boyfriend, as it turns out the two timing Nate Parks, in the episodes *Sense and Sense Ability* and *Necromancing the Stone*, Norman cleaned up fairly well and offered a slightly sinister twist to the tale.

On the personal front, the relationship between Norman and Helena had turned sour. There was no outlandish tabloid headlines, no reported affairs on either side and no physical or verbal abuse. Quite simply, by 2002, the long periods apart in their respective busy lives had drained the relationship of any passion.

Norman and Helena were quite calm about deciding to break up. They agreed that they still loved each other, just not in that way anymore. If such a thing was possible, Norman and Helena had smiles on their faces and a sense of relief when they decided that enough was enough. But they were not ready to announce it to the world. They had a child together and they were concerned that a sudden rush of tabloid scrutiny, complete with the requisite fabrications and gossip, might negatively impact Mingus.

And so the couple agreed to just keep it under their hats until they had a chance to explain the situation to their son and get him used to the idea that his parents loved him and would always be in his life. For the better part of six months, Norman and Helena lived their lives as normal as possible. Norman would flit in and out between jobs and, now that Mingus was older, Helena was once again finding her way in the working world and had moved her base of operations to New York. There would be shared custody centering around each other's work schedules. It all seemed so civilized.

The soon to be ex couple were kind and reassuring in explaining to Mingus the new situation as only a four year-old could understand it. The child would ask a few questions and his parents would patiently answer them. They most likely sighed a collective sigh of relief when it appeared that Mingus was taking their separation well.

Finally in the early months of 2003, the breakup was made public. Norman was once again a single man.

CHAPTER ELEVEN
ON THE MARKET

Typically Norman, but perhaps not typical of most actors post celebrity breakup, Reedus admitted to being both happy and contemplative about being single after coming out of the longest relationship he ever had. He had nothing but good things to say about Helena.

"She's an amazing woman, incredibly intelligent and fun," he told *The Sydney Morning Herald*. "She knows what she wants and she goes after it. She's a successful, powerful and intelligent woman and a really great mom and role model for Mingus."

For his part, fatherhood as a single parent, despite having been in his son's life since birth, entailed a bit of a learning curve. "When Mingus was smaller it was a little harder with him going back and forth between two places," Norman told *The New York Post*. "The only hard part was trying to figure out where his clothes were, at her place or mine."

Catering to a four year-old's whims also proved to be on the job training. There was the day when Mingus told his father that he wanted a black cat. Norman, by this time firmly wrapped around his son's little finger, scoured the better part of New York City before finding the perfect candidate, an angry, hissing, unkempt ball of fur that Mingus would name Eyes in The Dark.

But through the trials and tribulations of his first year as a truly single father, Norman was a truly happy man. "I'm really enjoying being a father," he said in a *DaddysCool*.com item. "I love that I run toward that [fatherhood] every opportunity I can get. I've learned patience from him [Mingus]. He doesn't freak out about anything. He's always so cool, calm and collected."

Well as cool, calm and collected as any four year-old can be. Norman told *Fugue* that there's definitely a ying and yang when it comes to Mingus. "I want him to grow up knowing that he's the shit," he said. "Sometimes he pisses me off. He'll throw something across the room or keep me up all night. But then he'll wake me up and say, 'I love you like the ocean.' And so you get up and do it all again."

Bottom line, Norman was a changed man. And according to comments made in *Content Mode*, he was also a much calmer one. "I laugh a lot now. I head bang harder. Things are silly and brilliant now, all at once. I don't really get upset when I come across fuck faces anymore."

Following his official break up with Helena, it did not take long for the tabloid press and the entertainment blogs to run rampant with speculation of how long it would be before Norman was once again dating and seriously involved. Norman laughingly denied the rumors, saying that he was not seeing anyone but offering his blueprint for any woman he might eventually be interested in. He offered that he was always looking for honesty and a lack of jealousy, as well as a sense of humor and a desire to have fun and explore new things.

However in Norman's world, there seemed to be little time for love. He was continuing to work at a maddening pace, literally jumping from film to film, which led many to speculate that, despite a filmography longer than the proverbial arm, the by now 36 year-old actor truly needed the money. The reality was that Norman had done, primarily small, independent, direct-to-video type films that were not paying much. So while Norman was living a comfortable lifestyle in the East Village, the fact of the matter was that he was living paycheck to paycheck. But, once again, owing to his own attitudes and creative leanings, he was forgoing any big budget studio offers while continuing to work in the salt mines of primarily B movies.

At the very least *Until the Night* appeared to have offered Norman a chance to showcase his dramatic chops. In this dramatic character study, Norman portrays a struggling and depressed writer who takes up with an ex-lover who is now married to a down on his luck actor. As the affair progresses, confusion and psychological obsession take over. Unfortunately what apparently, according to those who have seen the film, was a reasonably good performance by Norman once again went by the wayside and was quickly reduced to direct-to-video status and obscurity.

To those who had covered his career to that point, *Until the Night* seemed yet another questionable choice by an actor who, no matter what creative satisfaction he was getting, was teetering on the brink of falling into the trap of many actors who will do anything for a paycheck at the expense of their career.

Norman went globetrotting for his next role as a German police officer in the crime thriller *Antibodies*. He recalled in a *Suicide Girls* interview that he had been in Copenhagen when he got a call from a future good buddy Christian Alvart. "The director, Christian Alvart, contacted me when I was in Copenhagen. He flew there to meet me for a film he was doing called *Killer Queen*. Part of the financing team for *Killer Queen* also put together the money for *Antibodies* so he asked me to be a part of that as well."

By all accounts, Norman was able to pull off that very Germanic look and, if stills from that movie are any indication, he filled out the uniform fairly well. What is definitely known is that Norman and Alvart got along very well and the seeds of a future friendship were planted. While *Antibodies* managed to get some traction overseas, it would go down as yet another Norman vehicle that not a whole lot of people saw worldwide.

Norman moved up a notch in his next project, *The Notorious Bettie Page*, a biographical look at the life and times of the 50's pin-up girl. For Norman it was an easy in and out job; four days and only a handful of scenes as Bettie Page's abusive, jealous husband. In fact, despite some critical notices and a fairly brief theatrical release, *The Notorious Bettie Page* was a complete blur to the actor as he explained in a *Suicide Girls* interview.

"I kind of forgot that I did that movie. I just did it and then jumped into some other things. Then the movie comes out and this friend texted me from the theater and goes, 'Dude, you just bitch-slapped Bettie Page.' "

When he was not making films, Norman was never far from his art. With some fellow New York artists he formed a creative/supportive arts collective that would make art in various mediums and conceits and exhibit them. "The people involved were all very creative and we worked together on art shows and creative gatherings. I was doing a lot of photography and video installations. I always liked doing that kind of stuff."

Norman's search for the next creative challenge brought him to *Comfortably Numb*, a totally obscure comedy/adventure outing that was so below the radar that the only thing most historians know is that he was in it. But continuing good press, much of which being based on the fact that *The Boondock Saints* had finally caught on as a word of mouth video sensation that would ultimately surpass $50 million in sales, had magically given Norman a high enough profile that he would be invited to Germany to receive an award. Norman looked at the trip as an opportunity to hang out with friends he had made and to do a bit of sightseeing.

What he had not counted on was that Berlin would, physically and emotionally, change his life.

CHAPTER TWELVE
SCARS

Norman lay in the Berlin Hospital following the 2005 crash. His visitor's list was zero, with the exception of his *Anitbodies* director, Christian Alvart, who would stop by on occasion and became the defacto translator of German to English and back again between Norman and the doctors. "Christian sat at my bedside and translated back and forth," he said in a *Fielding on Film* interview. "We became good friends. I'd do anything for him.

Alvart also did his best during those visits to encourage him to think positive. But Norman, during and after the operations that put his face back together, was left largely to his own thoughts.

Thoughts that started at bleak and went steadily downhill from there.

Not surprisingly Norman, who had often described the first time he saw himself in a mirror as looking like *The Elephant Man*, felt his life and career were over. "My whole head was like hamburger," he stoically told *Entertainment Weekly*. "I thought, 'I'm never going to be an actor again. This is over.'"

The quick hop to Los Angeles to film *Meet Me in*

Marc Shapiro

Berlin had ultimately done little to boost his spirits and once back in Berlin, he felt he had to do something to get his mind right. If acting was not to be in his future, perhaps directing might. Aided by a package of toy soldiers, Norman spent hours manipulating the toys and first imagining and then writing down numerous camera angles. Before he knew it, a stack of rough script pages had begun to pile up at his bedside. Norman sent the pages to a friend in Los Angeles who encouraged him to try something once his hospital stay was over.

Norman was not sure but, upon his release from the hospital in July 2005, he made his way to Los Angeles where, over a short period of time and still showing the signs of the head on with the truck, he would attempt some creative therapy. The three short films that resulted were as dark as they were surreal in tone.

I Thought of You took the viewer inside the brain of legendary jazz musician Miles Davis. *The Rub* took a psychologically ugly look at the listlessness of anonymous sex. And finally Norman interpreted the concept of identity in *A Filthy Little Fruit* as a failed comedian suddenly suffers an identity crisis. By all accounts, Norman was alternately tentative and competent while directing for the first time and would ultimately, in a *Tumblur* interview, consider this personal exercise a success.

"They are three very strange short films which are all completely different," he said. "I directed, shot and edited them myself. I just sort of jumped in and I really enjoyed it."

But the joy would be short-lived. Although the doctors in Berlin had done an excellent job in putting Norman's face back together, the healing process would take time and Norman was still faced with looking in the mirror each day and seeing his less than perfect self. And as he explained to *Fielding on Film*, it was not a good time physically and emotionally for him.

"After the accident, I was totally self- conscious. My face was still swollen and I looked like I had a black eye. My equilibrium was off and I would trip over curbs. I was so not myself. I was terribly afraid."

So much so that Norman went into an emotional shell for some time. Acting roles came his way but he was reluctant to put himself out there with his face still battered. But the isolation from acting would end when legendary horror filmmaker John Carpenter made him an offer he quite literally could not refuse.

Carpenter, the godfather of modern horror based on a long litany of films that included the original *Halloween* and *The Thing*, was doing an anthology horror series for television entitled *Masters of Horror* and had an episode, *Cigarette Burns*, coming up that centered on the search for an obscure film that reportedly had only been seen once and had caused a violent reaction in the viewers. The lead, an emotionally scarred theater owner who is enlisted to find the film, seemed to have Norman's sensibilities written all over it. Norman was not sure but Carpenter insisted, literally giving him a boot in the ass to do it. The actor finally agreed his future as an actor might well hinge on his getting in front of the camera on *Cigarette Burns* and agreed.

Cigarette Burns would prove to be a tour de force of an acting experience. Norman's character was constantly walking a physical and psychological tightrope. In Carpenter's hands, the scares were both mental and visceral. In the best possible way, Norman would reinforce his acting chops with his ability to magnify pain and struggle in a totally believable and horrifying way. In hindsight Norman looked on *Cigarette Burns* as his way out of his own fears and into the world of a true fright master.

"You're with him [Carpenter]," Norman reminisced about the experience with *Shock 'Til You Drop*. "You're covered with blood. You're hanging out with [co-star] Udo Kier. It's surreal. You go to work with him [Carpenter]. One minute everything is subtle and then, suddenly, Udo Kier is ripping out his entrails and feeding them into a film projector. You pick up on all the nuances. It's an interesting world to be in."

The experiment with Carpenter was a success. The patient lived. And as his face slowly but surely healed up, Norman was back to work. Admittedly it would be baby steps. He played a character, coincidentally named Norman, in a television pilot entitled *13 Graves* that was not picked up and went under the name Henry Flesh in a short film called *Walls*. Norman went to France to film a fairly engrossing but rarely seen bit of French noir in *A Crime* in which Norman plays a man obsessed with finding the killer of his wife and encounters abrupt psychological turns along the way. Part of the attraction for Norman in *A Crime* was most certainly the opportunity to play opposite well-known actors Emmanuelle Beart and Harvey Keitel.

Well into 2006 and into 2007, Norman seemed to be back on his creative feet with the likes of *Killer Queen*, *American Gangster*, *Moscow Chill* and *Hero Wanted* offering a lot that appealed to Norman but also a lot that would ultimately go largely unseen. He also did a guest shot on the television series *Law & Order: Special Victim's Unit* which, by contrast was seen by the masses.

If there is a sleeper in this dearth of Norman appearances during this period, it most certainly is the starring role in *Moscow Chill* in which Norman plays an American hacker brought to Russia to commit bank fraud who finds himself up to his eyebrows in the violent Russian underworld. It is a solid bit of business, acting wise, as Norman shows he can play action hero with the best of them.

His lone brush with notoriety during this period being a minute long appearance in the aforementioned *American Gangster* (what many consider his first appearance in an A list movie which was directed by Ridley Scott and starred Denzel Washington and Russell Crowe.) Norman's on screen participation was limited to approximately one minute in a scene with Crowe in a morgue. His screen credit listed Norman as Detective In Morgue.

When asked, Norman would regularly site boredom as the reason he worked so much, which seemed to satisfy most. But he was getting leery of the inevitable question of why he seemingly does nothing but dark, intense and often violent roles. When that question was asked by a reporter from *Scene B. Seen*, Norman once again bristled at the question.

"I seem to do a lot of dark roles," he groused, "but I'm not really that dark. I'm so tired of everyone thinking I'm so dark. What it is is that I get upset easily and understand being upset. For me it all comes from a place of unhappiness. But I don't practice that in my life.

"I try to be happy."

CHAPTER THIRTEEN
NORMAN DOES SICK

And happy going into 2008 meant Norman spreading his wings on any number of personal and professional fronts.

In an effort to find an outlet for marketing his own creative efforts, Norman formed his own production company called *Big Bald Head*. Initially it was in response to a growing interest in purchasing his three short films (the proceeds of which would go to charity) as well as his more artistic photography (which would soon come to light in a coffee table-sized book).

With the aid of fellow New York artists, he would open a gallery in the heart of New York's famed Bowery called Collective Hardware. Norman would look back fondly at Collective Hardware (which closed in 2010) in a *Wall Street Journal* conversation when he proudly stated, "We had all the ingredients to make great art there."

Personally, having his son in his life was turning Norman to different avenues of expression. He learned how to cook and he decided to try being a vegetarian. But, most importantly, Norman had developed into the ideal father, equally a big brother, who despite his busy schedule was good about shutting it all out when Mingus was in the house.

"When I come here [New York], I'm with my son," he explained to *The Wall Street Journal*. "I'm just daddy when I'm in New York."

And while insisting on living in New York continued to insulate him from what he considered the inconvenience of cattle calls and auditions, Norman, thanks in large part to the due diligence of his management, who subconsciously went out of the way to automatically get him work that seemed to perpetuate the dark and dour image he had cultivated, was seemingly never out of work for very long. Such was the case when a script with the title of *Red Canyon* ended up on his doorstep. On the surface this tale of family members returning to their isolated home town to clear up some long kept mysteries and secrets, gave off the generic vibe of low-grade slasher horror. But given Norman's attitude toward the dark side, there was an immediate fascination for the character of Mac as he explained during an on set interview.

"Mac makes Crystal Meth. He's a sex freak. He's a rapist. He's a murderer. He's the bad guy."

As the script read, Norman had visions of the cult terror *Henry: Portrait of a Serial Killer*, one of his all-time favorites. "I liked how it sort of went for it. In every film, I've pretty much killed somebody. But this one was really, really rough."

While Norman was reading the script for *Red Canyon*, his agent, Rachel, was also reading the script in Los Angeles. Norman recalled the conversation they had the next morning during an on set interview. "The next morning my agent, Rachel, calls and says, 'Did you read that?' and I go 'Yeah.' And she goes 'That's the sickest fucking thing I've ever read in my life. What do you think?' and I go, 'Let's do it.' "

The only thing Katie Maguire knew about Norman was that a couple of her friends who were big fans of *The Boondock Saints* "were very excited that I was going to be working with him." Maguire, a veteran actress/writer/producer whose web series LI Divas is currently in its second season, was playing her first lead role in *Red Canyon*. It was the first time she had a trailer. And she recalled, in a 2015 interview with this author, that the buzz about Norman from her friends only escalated once she arrived at the isolated Utah location for the 30-day shoot.

"Norman was set to arrive a week after filming started but I remember before he arrived there was a lot of buzz around him and that the producers were very excited. And I was thinking, 'Oh my god! I wonder if he is like this character who is a grungy, nasty guy. Once I met him and started talking to him it was like, 'okay now I get it.'

What Maguire 'got' was that Norman was "lovely and very down to earth. He was a little shy and, if anything, a little quiet. But we weren't in any social situations and so he seemed pretty comfortable."

The actress related that Norman had come to *Red Canyon* straight off another shoot and appeared to be "sick." But that did not stop the director from putting Macguire and Norman to work on what would be the climactic scene in the film. "The first scene we shot together was one of the final scenes in the movie where he's trying to rape my character. I run after him, grab him, let him know that he's not going to do that to me and then [spoiler alert] both of us plunge off a cliff to our death. Norman was in the bathroom a lot during the filming of that scene. He was very sick with Strep Throat. But all the while we were shooting that scene he was very sweet and was worried that I might get sick."

When not filming, Maguire recalled that, "In between takes I would be sitting with him at a picnic table and we would be chatting about a lot of things. He would talk a lot about his son Mingus. Sometimes I would come up to him and he would be listening to some music on his iPad and he would give me headphones so that I could listen."

Norman also was quite the diplomat when it came to working with *Red Canyon's* inexperienced director. "There was no diva in him and he never got into it with the director. He was pretty humble about it all. He would show up, do his work and chat with whoever was around."

Norman dialed it down a notch following *Red Canyon* with a pair of short film appearances. In *Dead Line*, he plays an ex-con who is about to get even with an abusive prison guard and a bit in a horror short/send up called Clown that ultimately turned into a full-length feature. He would also appear in the role of a recording studio engineer in the well-received bio pic *Cadillac Records*.

Another 2008 effort, the supernatural horror sequel *Messengers 2: The Scarecrow*, was the inevitable follow-up to the fairly successful original. The film was going the direct-to-video route from its inception but it did offer up the rare opportunity for Norman to play the flat out lead, and a good guy to boot, as a farmer trying to save his family from ruin by seeking the aid of a supernatural entity. Creepy stuff ensues. But the movie was a largely critical success, due to Norman's ability to channel a solid, albeit edgy, hero in the face of terror.

By the end of 2008, Norman had arrived as a full-fledged working actor and his life as a single father, if you discount the stresses of going to parent/teacher conferences and watching as his chess protégé son constantly beat him at the game, was fulfilled.

As an artist, his reputation had garnered international popularity and, when not working on a film, he was inevitably off to some far-flung part of the world to appear at an exhibition of his work.

But Norman, at his most restless and impatient private moments, would often succumb to the frustrations of the business and, for him, the inevitable shortcomings. It also must have weighed on his psyche that he was fast closing in on 40 and, while he had settled fairly comfortably into the idea of being a working actor, he was nowhere near being an established A list star. He had acknowledged on several occasions how what he perceived as good work being undone by directorial and commercial interference.

In feelings first revealed in *GQ* and subsequently picked up by *US* and countless other outlets, Norman acknowledged his frustration. "I was definitely becoming a little down on it. I don't know if I was going to give up but, to be honest, I wasn't enjoying it as much. I had been in a few films where I thought we were going in this direction and then, after the editing and the music were put together, it was sort of going in a different direction I didn't feel so connected to."

The fact that being stereotyped in every movie as somebody who kills somebody made for good talk show and interview yucks had not deterred Norman from a serious desire that to break the stereotype and do a romantic comedy might actually be an interesting change of pace.

In a conversation with *GQ,* he revealed that in 2001 he actually had the opportunity to do just that handed to him on the proverbial silver platter as the boyfriend to Jennifer Love Hewitt in the romantic comedy *Heartbreaker*.

"When they came around, my agents at the time were like, 'They like you for the part and it's a Jennifer Love Hewitt movie.' And I'm like, 'Well what do I do?' And they're like, 'You're her boyfriend.' And I'm like, Well, do I rape her? Do I kill her? What do I do? And they go 'You're her sweet boyfriend.' And I was like, 'Absolutely not.'

"But yeah I just assumed that I would have to rape and kill her."

CHAPTER FOURTEEN
I LIVE FOR PAIN

It was a well -known fact that Norman rarely said no. And if a request came from somebody he considered a friend…well you get the picture. Enter Paul Sampson, a close acquaintance from way back in the day with an offer the ever loyal Norman could not say no to.

A part in a little ditty called *Night of the Templar*.

As he explained in a 2010 interview, friendship and loyalty went a long way in his decision. "Paul Sampson is an old friend of mine and he just asked me to do it."

Night of the Templar begins 700 years in the past when a medieval knight is betrayed by his advisor and some less than trustworthy cohorts. With his dying breath the knight curses those who crossed him to ten decades of excess before he will return to take his revenge on their descendants.

The premise and execution appealed to Norman in a very 70's, Euro trash horror kind of way, stylistic and outrageous all in one film. The actor was also drawn to the opportunity to play among such top line actors as David Carradine (who as fate would have it would die shortly after completing the film), Udo Kier and Billy Drago. *Night of the Templar* would be a project that, owing to the do-it-yourself attitude of filmmaker Sampson, would film over fits and starts over the next two years and would be one that Norman would look forward to returning to. Especially in the guise of sex addict Henry Flesh (yes the same moniker he used in a previous short film) who at one point in the film reprises his sequence from *Luster* by, once again, receiving oral sex on camera.

The very loose atmosphere on the set has become the stuff of urban legend, if you believe filmmaker Sampson, whose propensity for turning any serious question into a running stream of consciousness one-liners. "The vibe on the set?," he responded to a reporter for the Russian website *Dark Reel*. "How do I know? I was busy trying to make a movie. For me the vibe was hell, pure hell."

But Sampson managed to stay serious long enough to praise Norman not only for being a loyal, long-time friend but for being a big help in the nuts and bolts of the production, as he explained in *Dark Reel*. "Even when Norman is talking behind my back, he's got my back. We're good buddies in real life and on a lot of levels. Ultimately he would not have done the movie if there wasn't a level of respect between us. I know he didn't do it for the pay. He helped me get Udo Kier on board and, when the time came, he helped me get a PR person involved because he knew once the film was done I was going to need exposure."

It is safe to say that Norman came out of his shell while making *Night of the Templar*. According to reports, Norman's shyness in crowds and socially awkward nature, suddenly took a backseat to a swing for the fences macho guy as he was allegedly very 'out there' during the production and was, much in the same vein as Sampson, willing to swing for the fences, heavy on the sex, drugs and rock'n' roll surrealism when promoting the film.

In a *Village Voice* interview, Norman was quoted as babbling, "Yeah, sure I've got a big cock. Everybody knows that. Fuck! It's on my website! What was I talking about again?" Norman's mouth was in high gear when he told *Vanity Fair* that Sampson and he are good buds on and off the set. "Yep, we go out and get really fucked up and bang whores. What was the question again?" And finally *GQ* got an earful of Norman when he said, "Yeah me and Paulie [Sampson] will probably get fucked up the next time I see him, mass quantities of drugs and rock and roll."

As it would turn out, Norman's outrageousness was good for a laugh and did not ultimately put a dent in his reputation. In fact, indirectly, it may well have helped shine a light on the film as *Night of the Templar*, marginal release and all, opened to fairly decent reviews and, to this day, remains solidly in the camp of 'Cult Favorite.'

Norman next donned the identity of Dangerous Guy in *The Chase*, essentially a three-minute clothing line promo reel for a line started by his co-star Hilary Duff in which the actress is on the run from the bad guys but, conveniently finds time to regularly change into elements of her clothing line to throw off her pursuers. He also top-lined another short entitled *Syrofoam Soul* in which an older but hardly wiser character confronts his younger self in an attempt to come to terms with his life.

These short films may have well been the way Norman was winding down from the rigors of *Night of the Templar* and to keep busy while presumably waiting for the next big thing to happen. And that next big thing looming large on the horizon was the long anticipated sequel to *The Boondock Saints*, *The Boondock Saints II: All Saints Day*. Since the original film exploded as an internet and video sensation, hardcore fans of the film began to clamor for a follow-up and everybody connected with the first film were more than willing, in public comments, to fan the flames of bringing the MacManus's back to once again clean up the streets. And now, ten years after the fact, the sequel was finally going to happen.

Consequently nobody was more excited than Norman when it was announced that *The Boondock Saints II: All Saints Day* would be going into production late in 2008 for a reported theatrical release in 2009. "We were all excited when we heard the news," Norman enthused to *Cinema Blend*. "It was an on and off process forever and we were all just excited that it was really happening."

The return to *The Boondock Saints* had seemingly coincided with Norman finally turning the corner in his career. Although much of what he had done was still largely in the shadows and on the fringe, more and more his recent films were colored with the patina of mainstream and commercial. Despite his best efforts, Norman was now being seriously considered for major studio pictures. In the parlance of Hollywood, he was slowly becoming an "in-demand actor."

But being in demand was about to cause a definite conflict of interest. Longtime friend Christian

Alvart rang up with an announcement of his own; he was about to go into production on his biggest film to date, the science fiction movie *Pandorum* and had the perfect part for Norman. The only problem was that his film would go into production at the same time as *The Boondock Saints II*. Norman wanted to do both. So what to do? What to do?

"As it turned out, the producers of both films were friends and they were cool with working out the dates so that I could do both films," Norman told *Deadbolt*. "*The Boondock Saints* was being shot in Toronto at pretty much the same time that *Pandorum* was shooting in Berlin. So I was constantly bouncing back and forth between Toronto and Berlin and back and forth on little or no sleep the whole time I was shooting those movies."

The upside to *Pandorum* was he was not a star of the film and so does not appear all that much. But the downside was that around the time he began work on both films, he suffered a ligament tear in his right shoulder. And as he would offer, the little bits and pieces in *Pandorum* inevitably involved some 'heavy lifting.'

"In one scene I'm covered with oil and I'm hanging by my neck," he told *Deadbolt*. "Then there was another scene where I'm being yanked around by monsters. It was pretty grueling."

And, as recounted in *The Desk of Brian*, when Norman reported to the set of *The Boondock Saints II: All Saints Day*, things were not much better. "When I was on *Boondock*, I was screaming and shooting guns that must have weighed about 30 pounds each and that I was having trouble lifting and holding them. I was in a lot of pain on both sets."

"I thought I was going to die," he told *Cinema Blend*.

But all the pain he endured quickly disappeared on the set of *The Boondock Saints II*. Norman recalled that the toughest thing he had to do was relearn Murphy's Irish accent. Beyond that it was a surreal love fest, meeting old friends and welcoming new ones. That the script was very good and the production values were better was the icing on the cake of what was truly an emotional high for Norman. For the actor, it was a time to be comfortable and when it came time to promote the film, Norman was in bliss.

In an interview with *Dead Dave's Internet Radio*, the actor went all mushy when he said, "Just coming back and seeing all those old heads again, it was really fun. It was a good time." Norman was equally soft when he talked about the first day on the set with *Lost in Reviews*. "I remember the first day we started shooting, I saw Sean again for the first time in a long time and he says to me, 'Are we really finally doing this? Is this really happening?'" He was particularly grateful when explaining the vibe on the set to *A Pathetic Fangirl*, offering, "It was great. It was like working with your family. You're part of a group. You feel safe."

Once he got around that warm and fuzzy feeling, Norman also talked up the nuts and bolts of *All Saints Day*, channeling his impressionistic side in *It's Just Movies* when he understated that, "We knew that if we just did the same thing we did in the first one, it'll be there." He also acknowledged in the same conversation his admiration for director Troy Duffy's continued, straight-on approach to making the film.

"Troy's the kind of director who just knows what he wants. He's very much like 'Okay I want you to do this. You get in there and sort those motherfuckers out. They have killed this person. You're going to kill this guy.' "

Given all the good cheer, it was not surprising that Norman told anyone who would listen that he would do *Boondock Saints* movies as long as Duffy wanted him. But it was safe to say that the adrenaline was firing on all cylinders because, rather than taking some time off after completing the wall-to-wall action film, Norman immediately jumped into another film, albeit a more sedate one.

The Conspirator, directed by legendary actor Robert Redford, would be the initial production of Redford's The American Film Company. It is a straight-forward, character-driven account of the conspiracy surrounding the assassination of President Abraham Lincoln.

For Norman, it was the pedigree of the film that ultimately had him saying yes to the role of one of the conspirators, Lewis Payne, who would ultimately met his fate at the end of a hangman's rope. "It's Robert Redford first off," he told reporters at the premiere of the movie. "I would do a dog food commercial with Robert Redford. To play a piece of history is super interesting. The role I play has a lot of backstory. So yeah, of course, why wouldn't I do this?"

There were also several reasons why Norman agreed to do *Meskada*, a murder mystery set in an economically strapped town. One of the most obvious was that the movie was filmed in the Catskills which, for Norman, was a short train ride from his East

Village home. But, as he explained to reporters at the Tribeca Film Festival, there was more to it than that. "I liked the story. I like to be a part of an ensemble cast. I liked the actors involved. I liked the tone of the film and how the pace of the script went for more than just the message."

What seemed like less the message and more about exposure and a paycheck was Norman's appearance in the pilot episode for the return of the classic TV series *Hawaii Five-0*. That it was seemingly way too mainstream and pat for somebody with Norman's auteur tastes in projects did not dissuade the mercenary in Norman from taking the job. And while his career arc seemed to be drawing from progressively more mainstream interests, Norman would ultimately insist that he had an independent soul.

"I've worked on a ton of independent films," he reflected in a Tribeca Film Festival interview. "There's no money in it. But I like the idea of getting in there with a bunch of actors and just acting and hanging out."

In fact Norman wore Independence as a badge of honor, as he offered in *Complex*. "I never worried. I always worked. I never plotted out my career in any way. I didn't go for projects that would get me on the cover of *Entertainment Weekly*. But if a project came along that said 'circus midget' I was like 'Awesome! Let's go!' "

As it would turn out, Norman was on the verge of getting the best of both worlds.

CHAPTER FIFTEEN
NORMAN GETS DEAD

Norman Reedus was in a melancholy mood going into 2010. His relationship with his son Mingus could not have been better and the idea of being 'Dad' was a true bright spot in his life. His art, photography and his travels in those circles was a constant and positive stimulation. But when it came to his bread and butter, acting, he had just turned 40 and was not always happy with his lot.

"Acting in New York and Los Angeles had become such a grind and such a hustle," he candidly told *Flaunt*. "It was so up and down."

Norman also explored how his doing his best was often lost in the reality of the movie-making business and the fact that his world view had gone a little sour with age and experience in several conversations with *TV Guide*, *GQ* and *The Daily Mail*. "The constant rollercoaster nature of the business was getting on my nerves. A lot of the actors I was working with weren't on the same page."

But Norman had to work and so he went along with his agent's suggestion that he go to Los Angeles to attend the annual casting meat market for new shows called, often sarcastically, Pilot Season, reasoning that, if he got lucky, a regular paycheck and those all-important residuals from a hit show might perk up his spirits. Norman agreed.

"I just decided to go out to Los Angeles and try it out," he told *Complex*.

But Norman had it in his head that there would not be much during Pilot Season that would peek his interest on a creative and artistic level and, as he wandered the halls and gave perfunctory reads for anybody who thought enough of his unorthodox look to drag him into a room for an audition, he was coming away with lame promises of call backs and little else.

"It was like this big clusterfuck of actors and scripts," said a derisive Norman to *YRB Magazine*.

"I was reading tons of buddy-buddy sitcoms and series set in hospitals and police precincts," he told *Complex*. "Then there was this project about zombies called *The Walking Dead* that AMC was backing and Frank Darabont and Gale Anne Hurd were involved in. At that point I said, 'Forget all these other shows. What's this one?'"

The Walking Dead, based on the successful comic book series created by Robert Kirkman, Tony Moore and Charlie Adlard, premises a by now well-trod zombie storyline in which survivors of a zombie apocalypse band together to find shelter amid hordes of zombies (called Walkers) and the often more frightening humans they meet on their odyssey. Norman had never been what one would call a comic book geek but he knew his horror and, in *The Walking Dead*, he knew he had found something creatively stimulating. But by the time he got around to asking for an audition all the roles for *The Walking Dead* had been filled. Norman, however, would not be denied.

"I said, 'let me come in and audition for anything," he told *The Wall Street Journal*. He was ready and willing to get on the show in any way possible, even settling for an extra if that was all that was available. The producers admired his tenacity and had Norman read some lines from the pilot script, lines that were for a part that had already been cast.

"They had me read lines that went to Merle Dixon, a part that had already been cast with Michael Rooker," Norman recalled in *Timeout*. "I was told Merle was taken when they had me read Merle's lines, which led me to believe, 'Did he say no? Was he busy?'"

With the hint of a chance in the air, Norman, who by this time had already flown back to New York, got back on a plane and was soon back in Los Angeles. After the first read, he returned to New York and waited. What Norman would not realize at the time was that the producers were so impressed with the actor's audition that they wanted to take a second look. Norman was soon on his way out for another audition.

"I got a call and they said they wanted me to read some different lines of Merle's that were not in the pilot," he told *Timeout*. "So then I thought, 'Oh great! Maybe he's [Rooker] not doing it anymore, maybe I can get in and do it.'"

The reality was that Rooker was still in the cast and the producers remained so high on what they had seen from Norman that decided that they would create a new character that had not been in the pilot or the original comic book, Merle's younger brother Daryl.

Everybody connected with the show admitted that casting Norman as a brand new character this late in the process was an experiment at best. But it was one that they were willing to take. Norman would relocate to Atlanta where the first season, six-episode arc would take place. Being experienced with all manner of weaponry, Norman was only mildly surprised when he was told that Daryl's weapon of choice would be a crossbow which he managed to figure out in a couple of hours of practice

As it turned out, Norman would have some time to get acclimated to living and working in the South as his character would not be introduced until the third episode of the season. As portrayed in those early episodes, Norman seemed the stereotypical southern survivalist type, prone to simple-minded anger, violence and with a propensity for dropping a lot of F bombs and racist tendencies. To be fair, even in those early moments, there was a kind of primitive magnetism in his portrayal that seemed to work within the conceits of the show.

But rather than simply go along for the ride, Norman was quick on the trigger to producers and writers, insisting that there were deep trenches of character and emotion that would ultimately suit the character much better. Looking closer at the first season's episodes, one had to agree. Norman, even in the most dark and gory moments, was projecting vulnerability and a sense of insecurity and fear that had not been written into the scripts. Norman was playing with dimensions of character and emotion that quickly rang believable amid the zombie chaos and the producers and writers were thrilled to pick up on it.

Scenes that were being played less broad and more subtle by Norman went through without an attitude adjustment. The rest of the cast picked up on what Norman was up to and, subconsciously, began feeding off his vibe, making for more than the paper-thin characterization between the zombie action that many were expecting from the show.

Once the series was up and running, Norman would admit to *Digital Spy* and others that the transformation of Daryl from redneck caricature to flesh and blood human was essentially a voyage of self-discovery. "There was no source material for Daryl in the comic books or anywhere else. What I saw on the script pages that first day was Daryl saying 'fuck you!' and screaming his head off. I never had conversations with anybody on who Daryl is and so I kind of went with what my gut told me to be like playing this character. So I tried to play Daryl from the beginning with some sympathy."

In a bit of self-analysis that appeared in *Comicbookmovie.com*, Norman traced the evolution of Daryl through the first season. "Originally he was supposed to be this angry guy with a racist viewpoint and who hated everybody. You've seen him grow and become a better person. Daryl is this guy who needs a hug but, if you hug him, he'll try and stab you. He doesn't want to talk about his feelings but you can tell there's a lot of feelings bottled up."

Kirkman, in the same *Comicbookmovie.com* piece, was less subtle, giving Norman much of the credit for the show's success. "It all comes down to Norman. The way he has come in and taken over that role and defined Daryl Dixon. A lot of Norman's portrayal in the first season inspired our writers. We love writing him and we end up doing some cool stuff with him."

The Walking Dead filmed its first season from June through August 2010. And from the outset, Norman was literally in hog heaven. The day-to-day working experience was unlike anything he had experienced before. Norman was so enamored of the professional and personal relationship that had so quickly formed around *The Walking Dead* that he would often show up on days he was not scheduled to work just to watch the other actors bring what he described as "their A game." It was a period of near daily surprises as new script pages arrived every morning and Norman marveled at where the writer's minds were taking Daryl. But make no mistake, the first six episodes of *The Walking Dead* were a forerunner of what the series would quickly evolve into, an emotional and physical trial by fire in which everybody would happily work until they almost dropped before falling into bed with dreams of how exciting it would be to get up and do it all over again the next day. It was during those first episodes that Norman would join the ranks of the walking wounded with his first round of bumps and bruises.

Months before its October 31 premiere, the wheels were starting to turn. Not surprisingly, the horror press was all over the series and the cast from the outset, many of whom, like Norman, had worked in relative anonymity prior to *The Walking Dead*, were suddenly inundated with interview requests and invitations to horror media conventions and the first stints on the talk show circuit. Norman had always, even when flogging a totally obscure film appearance, proven generous when it came to dealing with the media. Always upbeat and accommodating, he was a publicist's dream.

And it was a good thing too, because from the word go *The Walking Dead* went from who knew to the pop culture phenomena of the year. The reviews were universally positive. The ratings, by cable standards, were huge and AMC, seeing they had the proverbial tiger by the tail, rewarded the show for an immediate pick up notice for 13 new episodes and a second season.

Even Norman had to mentally take a step back with the literal tidal wave of interest that *The Walking Dead* was generating. But once the shock of suddenly being recognized on the street had lessened, and being besieged by the first wave of paparazzi and autograph seekers had become more familiar, Norman morphed quickly into one of the most fan friendly and popular celebrities on the planet.

Helena had long known the erratic nature of an actor's life and had willingly adjusted her schedule to accommodate any extended absences by Norman. But in the midst of zombie fighting, he would always allow that he could not wait to get back to New York and spend quality time with Mingus who, at age 11, had become quite the little man and the perfect foil for his father. There was, most likely, the good-natured and often sarcastic banter between father and son. The times walking around the city and experiencing a leisurely lunch. Mingus had adopted many of Norman's eccentricities and artistic attitudes. Nothing in Norman's world inspired abject horror as much as it did curiosity and interest.

Mingus had already reached the stage where he had accompanied his father to gallery exhibits featuring his father's work. He was well aware that his father made movies and, most likely as his maturity level grew, was even allowed to see some of them. He was aware that his dad was doing a television series that had monsters and blood and violence and could hardly wait to see it. And he also had experienced the growing celebrity when people would come up to them when walking around town and ask to take a picture and exclaim how cool they thought he was.

Once while in Venice, Ca. they had run into a group of locals, one of whom had a *Boondocks Saints* T-shirt on. After the fact, Mingus would tell the person that they had his dad's picture on the shirt. For Mingus, everything about his dad was couched in cool.

But how that cool would impact his street cred was brought home around the time Mingus had turned 12, when the first episodes of *The Walking Dead* premiered and the mania was in full swing. "I picked up my son at school the other day," Norman recalled to *ComicBookMovie.com*, "and he had this big grin on his face. I asked him 'what are you smiling about?' He said some of the bigger kids at school had asked him…

"…Is your dad Daryl Dixon?"

CHAPTER SIXTEEN
NORMAN NEVER SLEEPS

If ever there was a time for Norman to figuratively stop and smell the roses, this was it. He had what every actor hoped for, security for at least a while. The hiatus would be perfect to reconnect with his son, friends and to do his art.

But rest and relaxation was not in Norman's vocabulary.

Which was why, with only a few days to kill before the start of filming on the first season of *The Walking Dead*, he agreed to do a star-studded 11-minute short about a family get together that suddenly makes a left turn involving Nazis and time travel entitled *Ollie Klublershturf Vs The Nazis*, which featured Chris Hemworth, Lainie Kazan, Rachel Nichols and George Segal. The film made a brief festival run before being released through an internet site.

And when old friend Christian Alvart came calling with essentially a cameo role at the bottom of the cast list, Norman could not resist, especially when it gave him an excuse to go to Germany for a few days. So if you happen upon the obscure *8 Uhr 28*, you'll find Norman in and quickly out of this romantic thriller comedy as The Stranger.

But ever the workaholic, the actor was looking for even more challenges.

"I was looking for something to do between *Walking Dead* [seasons],"he explained to *All In Films*. "I wanted something that was personable, low budget and that I could really get into it."

His agent, always willing to go the extra mile to keep his client happy and working, found something that he felt Norman would be up for, a horrifying bit of social, emotional and psychological reality called *Hello Herman*, the story of a put upon teen who goes Columbine, killing 42 people before being captured by the police. Just before the arrest, Herman contacts his favorite talk show host, Lax Morales with some video clips of the massacre and asking him to tell his story. For the ever mercenary Morales, the offer seemed like a sure ratings grabber but what he does not count on is that by agreeing to tell Herman's story, he is being forced to deal with his own demons. On paper the story seemed less of a Hollywood 'message' picture and more of a head on confrontation of the escalating level of random violence being perpetrated by young people and the underlying elements of bullying, video games and the seeming glorification of violence in pop culture and media. *Hello Herman* had controversy written all over it.

Originally, according to director Michelle Danner in a 2015 interview with the author, Norman was nowhere in the picture when it came to casting *Hello Herman*. "I was going to cast another actor friend of mine but he had a conflict with a series he was shooting. But it turned out that he had the same agent as Norman and he suggested 'How about Norman Reedus?'"

Danner took the actor's advice and sent the script to the agent who, in turn, sent Norman the script. "I read the script and I really liked it," he enthused to *All in Films*. "I was blown away. I couldn't stop thinking about it. I liked the subject matter of the script. I have a son who plays video games. It struck a chord with me."

Danner soon received a call from Norman's agent, strongly suggesting that Norman was interested in playing the role of Morales. However the director was cautious. "I didn't know a lot about him and I didn't want to get stuck with an actor in the lead role who would be difficult. So I set up a Skype interview with him. For me it was really an audition as well but I didn't tell him that even though I suspected he knew what was going on."

Danner reported that during the Skype session, they discussed the character he would be playing and they did some improvisational scenes. "I don't think he had ever worked the way I liked to work which was with a lot of backstory and improvisation. He was intrigued by that and that was part of the reason why he wanted to do the movie."

In the meantime, Danner did her due diligence and screened several of Norman's movies to get an idea of how Norman reacted in front of a camera. "I was impressed with his work in *The Boondock Saints*. He really understood how to work with his body."

For his part, Norman felt the slightest bit intimidated at Danner's sterling reputation as an acting coach as well as filmmaker. Norman had never been to an acting class in his life but actually contemplated taking some classes before filming began. Danner acknowledged Norman's uneasiness but put it in the best possible light. "Norman's training was his movies," she said. "He might have felt insecure because of the way I work. He might have felt that, because he had no formal training, he would be found out as a fraud. For him to have said that pointed to his basic humanity."

As it would turn out, Norman did not take any classes but *Hello Herman*, shot on a low budget, 19day schedule, was exactly what the actor was looking for, collaborative, freeing and in the spirit of the creative type of community Norman favored.

Danner related that Norman "had a lot of generosity of spirit and he brought his heart to the story." Her faith in the actor was immediately rewarded as the cameras rolled. "I was expecting a great performance and I got that. At that time, he had 40 films under his belt and he knew how to work in front of a camera."

And as Danner related, he was not shy about offering up his own ideas and suggestions. "He was incredibly creative and he had a lot of ideas and, in one instance, he saved my ass. He had an idea of how he wanted to shoot a scene and I had another idea. Because we had worked so well together to that point, I agreed that we would shoot both his idea and mine and, as it turned out, when I was in editing, that he had been right and that his idea worked best for the film."

But even as he worked on *Hello Herman*, the wave of sudden and unexpected opportunity continued to surround him. Exhibit A? A mid-production side trip to return to his music video roots in a very big way and with a very big star. Lady Gaga in a religious-themed video ringed with sexuality and bikers called Judas.

"I didn't have to audition," he told *Rolling Stone*. "I was in Los Angeles doing a movie [*Hello Herman*]. I had the weekend off and, as it turned out, my manager had been talking to Gaga and she asked if I wanted to do the video? I said, 'Fuck yeah, that should be fun.'"

Danner disagreed with Norman's version. "Norman deciding to do the music video really threw the production for a loop. He made us scramble and it was really difficult to accommodate that. One of the producers came up to me and said, 'You know you really don't have to let him do this. This is really messing you up.' And it did mess me up. One of the pivotal scenes in the movie was to be shot in a jail cell at four in the morning and, because Norman left, we didn't get it and had to go back and get it at a later date and shoot it. But I don't regret not saying no to Norman because I truly did not want to deny him that opportunity."

While excited about it, beyond having heard the song *Judas* and liking it a lot, how the video would play out was still a mystery to Norman as he offered in a *New York Post* interview. "They didn't tell me much beyond, 'You're Judas, the song is called *Judas*, Gaga is playing Mary Magdalene and another guy is playing Jesus. They asked me if I could ride a motorcycle and I ended up riding my own."

The *Judas* shoot lasted two days and, according to Norman, they were very long, beat-the- shit-out-of-you days, covering many locations and a lot of hours.

In one scene, Judas and his biker disciples, with Mary Magdalene along for the ride, got permission to close off a section of Los Angeles freeway. And while Norman would be the first to tell you that he does not have pretty feet, they insisted that viewers see Judas' real feet in the scene where Gaga washes them.

During the shoot, Norman came to respect Gaga. He saw the devoted Catholic who would begin the shoot by calling for a group prayer before charging headlong into *Judas'* very dark and profane take on religion and icons. And in the daring sequence in which Jesus and Judas prepare to make out, he also saw her as the queen of improvisation and said so in a conversation with *Rolling Stone*.

"I was going in for the kiss and then Jesus and I looked at each other like 'Are we going to make out? What's going to happen?' But then she runs over in that outfit and she goes, 'I've got an idea! I'm going to pull out this gold gun, one that shoots lipstick out of it, and then I'm going to put it on you.' Then she gave me a look like 'is that cool with you?' and I just said 'Rad!' So she said 'Great!' It was totally last minute."

After completing the video, Norman was literally on autopilot as he raced across town to put the finishing touches on *Hello Herman*. It had been a busy hiatus in which Norman, in his extended busman's holiday, was like a kid in a candy store, quite simply getting better at what he did. But Norman could tell that the temperature was beginning to turn. It was getting warmer, then it was getting hot.

Soon it would be time for Norman to return to his day job.

Among *The Walking Dead*.

CHAPTER SEVENTEEN
WHERE NORMAN LIVES

In the parlance of *The Walking Dead*, the consensus was that Norman was about due for a battle field promotion. Given that nobody had a clue what the response to Daryl would be, the producers had felt safe in easing Norman into the show as a 'recurring' character. But all that changed quickly when, by the end of the first season and, on the strength of a mere four episodes, it was announced that Daryl had joined the ranks of the main *Walking Dead* cast.

For Norman this would mean a logistical change. Whereas before he had felt comfortable flying in and out between his New York East Village digs and Atlanta, the fact was that the storyline from this point forward would necessitate filming in far flung, fairly isolated areas of Georgia. Throw in the second season increase from six to 13 episodes and Norman and the rest of the cast would now be faced with a seven month shooting schedule. Bottom line, Norman would need a second place to live while the show was in production.

While the majority of the cast were staying in Atlanta, Norman was inclined to take advantage of the relative isolation afforded by the outlying small towns and hamlets. By this time he had gathered a small armada of all-terrain vehicles and wanted a place where he could be alone with his thoughts, away from big city noise and to give his Triumph Scrambler motorcycle and a 1979 Ford F150 truck a workout in the Georgia back woods.

He found the ideal spot in a two-story out-of-the-way home in Palmetto, Georgia. It met all the requirements of Norman's feelings about being alone. The woods surrounding the home were thick and resistant to every sound but that of wildlife and the natural movements of nature. The landscape was dotted with numerous, winding backroads. Neighbors? If there were any to speak of, Norman would rarely see them. This was a lot of quiet for somebody who had spent most of his adult life in the hustle and bustle of big city New York. And it would be the contrary nature of the move that would give Norman pause.

"I think I was very nervous when I started [moved to Palmetto]," he admitted in a conversation with *The Savannah News*. "I'm more confident now. When I started [in New York] I was living in Chinatown and I was terrified of bugs. Now I'm in Georgia and I have tick bites all over me and I'm like 'whatever.'

As he became more acclimated to the small-town lifestyle, Norman would grow more comfortable with his surroundings and, either on his motorcycle or the recently purchased terrain friendly truck, would spend a good part of his free time tooling through the woods and the backroads, experiencing solitude on an existential level, for what many observers felt was the first time. "Riding through these little two lane roads with cows going by and the sun coming up and going down. It's really great."

The close proximity to *The Walking Dead* base camp for much of the second season filming was an added plus. Rather than arranging for a driver to pick him up and drop him off, Norman would simply hop on his motorcycle and do a leisurely ride to the set and then retrace his steps at the end of the day. Norman would find those moments on the road as an insight into the way people could be.

"I have an old truck with big wheels on it," he related to *AMC*. "What I've found out is that, if you ride in the country in a truck, the other truck drivers will wave at you. I just love the politeness down here."

Needless to say, the outlying regions of Georgia welcomed *The Walking Dead* Production Company with open arms. On a purely material level, it meant money and jobs. On seemingly a much deeper level it gave small town America a chance to showcase Southern hospitality. When they were out and about in the small towns, the cast and crew of *The Walking Dead* were greeted like conquering heroes as, even in the tiny hamlets, word had traveled fast that this show about zombies was a very big deal.

Norman was the ideal ambassador for the show. Always friendly and accommodating to people who came up to him on the street, always willing to stop, talk and pose for selfies and sign autographs, Norman was downright humble and real in the face of it all. "I get stopped all the time and 99.9 % of the people are great," he explained to *The Savannah News*. "I don't mind it [the attention] one bit. I'm very excited to be in this position."

He was also apparently excited to find female companionship along the way. Since he joined *The Walking Dead*, it had been regularly reported in the gossip and tabloid columns that Norman was constantly fending off the attention of flirting females, some reportedly zombie extras and some even reportedly coming on to Norman in full zombie make-up. But the rumors continued into the second season that Norman was seeing somebody during the show's second season. The only mention of it was in a 2011 *Digital Spy* interview in which the reporter described the scene 'with Norman pulling away from the set on his black Triumph with his leggy girlfriend sitting behind him.'

But Norman's sense of bliss, as well as the entire production of *The Walking Dead*, was about to be ruffled as the second season was about to go into production. *Deadline.com* got the rumors and speculation off to a flying start when it reported that Frank Darabont had fired the entire first season writing staff. Robert Kirkman soon went public to refute much of the story by saying that there would be some writing changes but that they would not affect the production of the show. Shortly thereafter it was announced that first season writer Glenn Mazzara had been hired as a writer/executive producer and would put together a reconstituted writing staff that included five more writers. One rumor on the writing front would have it that famed horror novelist Stephen King would be writing one episode of the second season. Finally *The Hollywood Reporter* stirred the pot when they broke the story that Frank Darabont had been fired as showrunner, allegedly for butting heads with

AMC executives over budget reductions, a basic clash of creative and business ideals and a lot of ego. *The Hollywood Reporter* piece included comments from cast members who insisted that their names not be used for fear that retaliation from the AMC executive suites might entail their character unexpectedly being killed off. After all, this was a show about zombies.

Norman was circumspect when questioned about how the changes were effecting the cast, speaking in near heroic terms as he explained how the cast responded by banding together, being super collaborative and just doing their best to make the show better. But finally he had to admit in a *Complex* interview that he really didn't have a clue. "I'll never really know what that was all about," he offered. "All that happened in offices where they have air conditioners. I don't even know how all of that works. I do know that Glenn [Mazzara] came in and was sort of put in a difficult situation and that he tried to make the best of it."

Making the best of it involved a radical departure from normal protocol when Mazzara began allowing the actors to sit in on writer's meetings and respond to questions from the writers on how their characters were reacting and interacting with other characters in certain situations. For Norman, this process would be a successful transformation from a Daryl, despite the subtle moves, that had been largely a 'fuck you, kick some ass redneck' to a much more layered and nuanced character. Even at this relatively early stage in his *Walking Dead* odyssey, Norman was regularly faced with the question of just who Daryl is and what he will become to the point of madness. In a *Digital*

Spy interview, he laid out the highly quotable and empty "I wreak havoc in Season 2" with a fairly succinct summation of where Daryl has been and where he sees him going.

"I wreak havoc for sure but there's also some sensitive moments as well," he said. "I like the mixture. I'm really interested in the concept of angels stabbing you in the back and devils crying and giving you a hug. I like the mixture so I'm really getting the opportunity to be ferocious. Daryl is like one of those guys who needs a hug but doesn't want anybody to watch. It's nice all the layers that I get to put in every day with every scene. I get to play with Daryl as much as possible."

With the storyline of *The Walking Dead* having moved from the relative confines of Atlanta, filming on the second season appeared to have a more guerrilla filmmaking feel to it as it played out in the woods and on the roads of Middle America. All the talk about budget cutbacks and shortened shooting schedules did not, at least on the surface, appear to be impacting the episodes. Character-wise, the show seemed to be constantly moving out of the box in terms of alliances, betrayals and suspicions. The zombie sequences remained the weekly treat, with truly horrific and well-choreographed bloody kills and fights. All of which played out like clockwork in an often stifling Georgia summer.

Cuts, scrapes, bruises, the occasional strains and broken bones continued to be a badge of honor among the returning cast members. And in that area, Norman had become the keeper of the castle when it came to judging when the second season's latest additions to the cast showed up on day one, as he explained in an interview with *AMC*.

"It's interesting. Because when the new people come on, I kind of look at them the way Daryl would look at them. I don't really talk to them. I kind of give them dirty looks. Then, after a couple of episodes, when they're all beat up, have scrapes all over their bodies and they're kind of walking as if they're 95 years old, then I open up and I'm like, 'Hey, nice to have you on board.'"

For Norman, the days and sometimes nights seemed to meld into a seamless whole. Every day, when he would pick up that day's script pages, there was inevitably a surprise or a challenge. He was good about doing press during filming but, reportedly, was more content to just hang out when not shooting and talking about everything not connected to *The Walking Dead*. His son would regularly pop up in conversation, as would his art. And when he was around Georgia locals, it was like one never ending lovefest, in which people from the area towns would ask Norman how their favorite redneck zombie fighter was doing. It was an aspect of working out in the boondocks that would, for Norman, form endearing memories.

But when he was on call, which was already evolving into big chunks of every episode, it had become a highly regimented and, by Norman's standards, orderly process. In fact, Norman was downright anal in several interviews, including *The Savannah News*, in chronicling what his *The Walking Dead* days were like.

"I get up and the sun's not up yet. I slam a cup of coffee. I get on my motorcycle and ride through the backroads of Georgia to the set. I have my eyes peeled so as to not hit any deer that jump out in front of me. I get to work and go into my trailer and change into my filthy clothes. I go into make-up and hair. There's usually some music blasting in the trailer. I get doused with filth, black slime and blood if a scene calls for it. Then everybody high fives each other and walks to the set. Everyone starts screaming and we get into this mode. Then we shoot a scene. That's pretty much how it goes."

Until it's time for Norman and the rest of *The Walking Dead* cast to clock out.

"We film eight hours a day. By the end of the day, all of us are walking back to our trailers, limping, holding our backs like we're 90 years old. Some people have fresh cuts on them that are real. I get back on my motorcycle, covered in blood, and I drive home. I jump right into the shower. The ring of dirt and blood on my shower floor is amazing to look at. My sheets are black and red from the stuff I couldn't wash off in the shower.

"In the morning, I throw the clothes in the washing machine, get back on the bike and go do it again."

CHAPTER EIGHTEEN
QUICK CHECK THE SCRIPT

The only deviation from that routine, for Norman as well as the rest of the cast, is the day they receive the script for the next week's show. The actors immediately skim through the pages, paying particular attention to the last few pages. There is a sigh of relief if they find that their character has not been zombie chomped or has gotten an arrow in the head and will live to fight another day.

Norman had a good laugh at a *Savannah News* reporter's suggestion that he might show up one day for work only to read a page that indicated 'Daryl gets an arrow in the head.' "I would be lying if I said that our entire cast, every time they get a script, doesn't race through to the end and heave a sigh of relief if they make it."

As it would turn out, Daryl would, indeed, make it through to the end of filming on the second season. And beyond as, on October 25,2011, the second season premiere of *The Walking Dead* broke all records for cable ratings in the all-important 18-49 demographic and was rewarded with an immediate pickup for Season Three and 16 additional episodes.

By that time Norman had returned to New York, suffering a bit of culture shock after seven months in Georgia, and was enjoying walking the streets of the East Village and spending a lot of quality time with his son. However the actor could not stay idle for too long and, as with the previous season's hiatus, was busy on other projects.

The most challenging and amusing included his first ever voice-over work as Frank Castle/The Punisher in the English language version of the Japanese Anime (direct to video) *Iron Man: Rise of Technovore*, a Marvel superhero mashup. Norman would often chuckle at the fact that playing Daryl with a distinct Southern lilt had slipped over into his voice-over work as The Punisher and had given the comic book anti-hero a bit of a down south twang. During his time off, Norman also had a chance to flex some on screen dramatic muscles in the down and out drama *Sunlight Jr.*, which starred Naomi Watts and Matt Dillon as a destitute couple whose already hard life was about to be further compromised by a pregnancy. Norman played a no good drug dealing ex-boyfriend who turns up and tries to get Naomi's character back into his life.

"The thing I liked about *Sunlight Jr.* was that it felt very real," he told *Vulture.com*. "For me it was like a very real, very honest portrayal of a family trying to hold it together. My character is a drug dealer but he doesn't take drugs. He's a lot more evil than that and very intimidating."

Norman's last official 'busman's holiday' project before returning to start filming on Season Three of *The Walking Dead* would easily be one of his more outlandish characters to date, a meth lab owner under siege in an all-star anthology goof fest anthology film called *The Pawnshop Chronicles*. For the record, Norman's character, Stanley, spends most of his time on film barely recognizable behind a gas mask. Norman explained that the disguise was his idea.

"In that movie you've got to look for me," he told *IFC.com*. "I wanted people to see me in that film and be like 'Is that so and so?' They [the filmmakers] kept asking me 'Can we see your face a little bit more?' And I'm just like, 'No. Not at all.'"

Given his many projects over the past two *Walking Dead* hiatuses, many observers of the actor have felt that Norman might well be hurting the show in some way by doing so much during off-season time. In a conversation with *Daily Dead.com*, the subject was broached and Norman was fervent in support of *The Walking Dead* and insisting that he is not overdoing it with off-season projects.

"Sometimes I'll do somethings between seasons but I want to put 100% into this," he declared. "When you're on a show that's a hit, people tell you that it's your chance and to do everything that comes your way. But I've said no. It wouldn't be fair to all the people I work with on *The Walking Dead* if I spread myself all over the place."

But when a deal was struck with game makers Activision for a first person shooter *Walking Dead* video game involving the characters of Daryl and Merle, Norman was ultimately intrigued and signed on to voice Daryl in the game and, most importantly to him, to sign off on dialogue and storylines.

May 31st was the official start of filming on

Season 3 of *The Walking Dead* as cast and crew members returned to the familiar outdoor Georgia locations. There were a lot of handshakes and hugs and 'how's the family? and 'what have you been doing?' small talk. But it only took premiere episode director Ernest Dickerson's official call to the set for the first scene to let everybody know that *The Walking Dead* were back in business.

As with the previous season, the cast was being filled out by a handful of periphery new characters and, most importantly to Daryl, the return of big brother Merle and other characters missing from the show since Season One appearances. As the scripts began to unfold, the building blocks of Daryl's character were being added to.

Still the quiet outsider, there would be signs that Daryl would be taking on, albeit in a subtle manner, more of a leadership role in the group of survivors and, by association, putting him at odds with the defacto leader Rick whose psychological resolve was beginning to crack by the end of the previous season and who would further unravel in the current season. Also adding to the tension was the growing nature of the relationship between Norman and Carol. From the moment Daryl appeared on the show, there had been growing speculation, primarily in fandom, as to when Daryl would experience zombie love with one of *The Walking Dead's* female survivors. It was also obvious that the return of Merle would force Daryl to deal with certain issues.

The actor acknowledged in a *Daily Dead* interview that he's excited that Daryl is finally stepping out of the box in terms of character development. "He's tighter with the group and he doesn't feel like such an outsider. People are relying on him and he's finding comfort in that."

Norman was extremely stoked when a reporter for *IGN.com* asked him about how the Daryl/Merle relationship would pick up in Season Three, acknowledging that the return of big brother would be a large part of the new season and that it would be complicated. "You find out reasons why there is even more conflict than you assumed between them. But there's also the heartache and the situations they've gone through and those things bond them as a duo."

But ultimately it is the possibility of the Carol/Daryl relationship that was looming largest in *Walking Dead* fandom, a question made all the more prominent with the speculation mounting that Daryl is either gay or a virgin and that the show has plans on addressing one or both issues at some point. Depending on when the question had been broached in the past, Norman could be either frivolous or serious in responding. Right around the time the third season was just getting into gear, Norman was a bit of both when talking to *IGN.com*.

"I just think it's more interesting to have these two people see something kindred in each other and gravitate toward each other in that way. It would just be too obvious if we made out and we were a couple. It's been done and I want to do stuff that is different on this show. Besides, I don't think Daryl is the type of guy who has game. I don't think Daryl is that suave. I think if anyone made moves on anyone, Carol would make moves on Daryl and Daryl would probably just prematurely ejaculate in his pants and go hide in the bushes."

Through the fall and into the winter months, Season Three of *The Walking Dead* had truly hit its stride. The character arcs were running deep and divergent at every turn and Norman may well have been the most satisfied actor on the set seeing how far and how creatively Daryl could really go. If anything, the zombie action was crisper and more polished, having effectively transformed from an easy point of attraction to the show into, often, a solid adjunct to the constantly shifting storylines of the humans.

Typical of Norman's nature, the actor was literally throwing himself into every scene. Consequently Season Three was conspicuous by the fact that Norman made more trips to the hospital than he could remember but did recall in a *Grossly Hardcore* interview that two of his more memorable trips to the ER were for a torn rotator cuff in his right shoulder and a badly twisted knee.

By late November, with still half the season's episodes left to shoot, showrunner Mazarra announced that the season finale would be directed by Ernest Dickerson.

Not long after that announcement AMC issued a press release indicating Glenn Mazarra would be leaving his position with *The Walking Dead* once the season was completed. In the wake of Mazarra's dismissal, the speculation returned that the AMC brass and the creative side of *The Walking Dead* team were constantly in chaos and that the bickering would ultimately impact on the quality of the series. But as the cast and crew soldiered on with a lame duck showrunner through the remaining episodes of the third season, Norman pretty much summed up the attitude of the cast and crew in the midst of this latest change at the top in an interview with *Rolling Stone*.

"It brings the cast and crew together because we fight for the show," he said. "We fight to keep it real. We fight for the story. We fight for each other. We know we have a good thing going here."

CHAPTER NINETEEN
THE ATTACK OF THE BIG BALD HEAD

Despite the behind the scenes controversies, the third season of *The Walking Dead* would turn out to be the best to date and easily confirmed the show's status as the most popular series both in the US and abroad. Consequently for the cast, who had already achieved superstar status in the eyes of many by the end of the second season, the third had driven the actor's status to manic proportions.

In particular Norman, who had been a constant on the pop culture and comic con circuit since he took on the role, was now having to resort to wearing a disguise. At one such Comic Con, Norman took to wearing a panda bear mask every time he wanted to walk the convention floor or even go to the bathroom. It would fool people but, to Norman, it would prove to be a surreal experience.

With the overwhelming ratings success, AMC was quick to pull the trigger on a fourth season, 16 episode schedule which would begin filming on May 6, 2013. With, surprisingly no film roles on tap during the hiatus before Season Four would begin, Norman was suddenly a man of leisure. Much of his time was spent back in New York with Mingus and reconnecting with old east coast friends.

But he would also take time to take some pictures.

Norman was old school when it came to his photography. He had long since adopted the habit of carrying a camera with him everywhere he went. And while most photographers lived and died by a particular brand of camera, Norman had no allegiance to any one brand. Already an avid artist/photographer of the dark and bizarre, his attitude, especially in the area of photography, would be further influenced by the horror vibe of *The Walking Dead* and the often desolate surroundings in Georgia.

On his recreational rides through the Georgia woods and during his rides to and from the set, Norman would regularly come upon roadkill in various degrees of decomposition and deterioration. He became fascinated by the often flattened and distorted carcasses and, in particular, the seeming sadness in the eyes of the dead animals. He began photographing the more interesting roadkill and soon brought the entire *Walking Dead* cast and crew into his photographic obsession.

He told *Co Create,* "I would text the cast, 'Hey it's Norman. If you guys find any good roadkill on the way to the set, be sure to remember where it was so I can go back and photograph it."

His obsession with the dark side as well as his notoriety with *The Walking Dead* resulted in an invitation in November 2011 to put some of his photos in a Times Square charity exhibit and sale for the anti-poverty organization Oxfam. The organizers suggested some informal shots from the set of the show as well as pictures from the surrounding Georgia countryside. Norman knew that the production would not allow any shots from the set. But he had another idea.

Roadkill.

"I ended up taking all these shots of roadkill and what I saw every day," he told *The Hollywood Reporter.* "I try to see things in a different light. So that was sort of the theme without there being a specific theme."

However the organizers of the charity exhibit were not too thrilled with Norman's choice of subject matter, citing the fact that this was the holiday shopping season in New York and that his artistic direction might well put people in a depressed mood. But Norman persisted in his vision of roadkill and would be rewarded when every one of his photos sold within the first hour.

Since he formed *Big Bald Head*, his publishing and charity oriented merchandising arm in 2008, Norman had seen his creative efforts grow in proportion to his progress as a worldwide celebrity. But as somebody who rarely had any free time, the mechanics of running *Big Bald Head*, essentially a one-man operation, was beginning to be a bit time consuming and a gradual learning curve. With his three short films he would originally burn them onto DVD's, package them and then trudge down to a local Chinatown post office and stand in line to mail them. With individual photo requests, it meant going to a printer, printing up the photo and then shipping it. Eventually Norman became more techno-savvy when he realized that he could have people download his merchandise from his website. Problem solved.

117

However the creative side of Norman had always toyed with the idea of taking his art further afield and publishing a book of photos. "Everyone had always asked me to do a book," he said in a *Tumblur* interview, "and in a way it sort of made sense. I have so many photos because I've gotten the opportunities to see things that I would not have seen otherwise. Finally, around the time *The Walking Dead* was churning out the first batch of episodes for season four, Norman was approached by the small independent publishing house, *Authorscape,* who approached him with the idea of putting out a book. Norman liked the independent nature of *Authorscape* and their dedication to producing quality, well-designed books.

"I said yes, finally," he told *The Hollywood Reporter*. "Let's do it."

Norman began the process of sifting through 16 years of photographic images, culled from his world travels as well as some more intimate and personal photos before coming up with the pictures that would fill out the 132 page hardcover collection called *The Sun's Coming Up...Like A Big Bald Head* that would be released, perhaps appropriately on Halloween 2013. A truly progressive thinking effort, the book paints Norman as somebody who is always observed who, through his photos, is now the observer. As a professional courtesy to singer Laurie Anderson, whose song *Sharkey's Day*, contained the lyrics 'big bald head,' Norman sent the final collection for her to look at in hopes that she would allow him to use 'big bald head' in the title of the book. Anderson loved the photos and readily agreed.

"It's very personal," Norman told *The Hollywood Reporter* of the collection. "The photos are through my eyes, like an interpretation of what my surroundings were at certain times. The photos are different things that I saw and kind of put my own personal little tweak on them."

Highlights of the collection were derived from *The Walking Dead* informal shots he managed to get by the production censors, a subtle but quite expressive shot taken in a Russian prison of two prisoners poking their heads out of a doorway as a small cat runs by, a bloody shot from John Carpenter's *Cigarette Burns* and, for a little contrast, some quite intimate and telling portrait style shots of his son Mingus.

Exercising his creative urges was always a welcome side trip from his day job as a zombie fighter in a ravaged world. But eventually it was time to scratch another itch as *The Walking Dead* returned from its mid-season hiatus and Norman was back to being Daryl…

…His crossbow in one hand and his camera in the other.

CHAPTER TWENTY
WHO'S THAT LADY?

The subject of Norman's status in the dating world had always been a hot topic, both on and off the screen. In the role of Daryl, he can't seem to get away from the idea that Daryl and Carol, two extremely damaged souls even by *Walking Dead* standards, are truly made for each other and should eventually become a romantic item while the zombie apocalypse rages all around them. Norman, in several interviews, holds out the possibility of that happening but always in a rather cerebral, psychological and in a way in keeping with their characters and their scarred psychies.

When it came to Norman's love life in the real world, Norman had always, good-naturedly side-stepped the question by saying variations on 'at the moment I'm single.' But since the by now 45 year-old actor found fame in *The Walking Dead*, there had been a lot to suggest that, as stealth as he would like to be, Norman had been spotted squiring a lot of ladies around town.

His first serious relationship since breaking up with Helena coincided with his landing the role of Daryl in *The Walking Dead*. She was model/actress

Jarah Mariano and there is photographic evidence that indicates they were in a 'serious' relationship for two years before going their separate ways. Reportedly Norman took a year off from any serious dating before a literal logjam of rumor, speculation and reality ushered in 2013.

The stories were hot and heavy for a while that Norman and his *Walking Dead* co-star Laurie Holden were dating. The speculation on this front were fueled by pictures taken at a *Walking Dead* roundtable discussion in which Norman walked up to Holden and gave her a long and lingering kiss on the mouth. Another picture that same night had Laurie reciprocating with a more than friends peck on the cheek.

Singer/actress and also a fellow *Walking Dead* cast mate Emily Kenney was also rumored to be in Norman's personal life but, ultimately, this one seemed to stop at the friendship level. Easily the most serious appearing relationship appears to be his current relationship with the much younger model Cecilia Stingley. Reportedly Norman and Cecilia have been more on than off since April 2013, long enough to inspire a slew of tabloid pregnancy/engagement rumors and a lot of paparazzi shots of the couple hand in hand at various events.

But to hear Norman say it, his legions of fans have been dreaming. "I'm so very single right now," he insisted to *Elle*," and I'm really enjoying it."

CHAPTER TWENTY ONE
DEAD 4 YOU

The days counted down to the May 6, 2013 start of filming on Season Four of *The Walking Dead*. And Norman had remained true to his 'no new parts' during his hiatus. There had been the usual empty rumors and speculations. It seemed like every time Norman mentioned a favorite TV show or filmmaker, the press was breathless with the notion that the actor just might be making an appearance. One of the more enticing possibilities was that Norman had said publically that he loved the television show *Portlandia* and would love to do an episode.

Norman finally did cave in, literally one day before *The Walking Dead* began production when he agreed to do a cameo as himself in the comedy/dark thriller *Stretch*. In it one of the lead characters stumbles into a room where a woman is found dead in a bloody bed just as a blood spattered Norman enters the scene and cracks subtle and wise.

Norman returned to *The Walking Dead* set in high spirits. The time off had given him a chance to emotionally breathe and to get away from being the constant center of the fan universe. New York continued to be a refuge, his long-time friends and the overall vibe of the city had served to insulate him from the public scrutiny. He was still able to walk the streets of his neighborhood and not be bothered. But it was easy for him to concede in a *Complex* interview that "It [the attention] was getting a bit taxing".

But truth be known, Norman really did not have a whole lot to complain about. He was on a hit television series and, going on 45, had been, ironically after more than two decades in the business, crowned the latest 'next big thing.' He had money. He had women. He had the life most people would kill for.

Season Four was shaping up to be a watershed moment for *The Walking Dead*. The characters were, after three seasons, pretty much set in stone as was the current stable of writer's familiarity with the entire Walking Dead concept and what could be done with it. Season Three had seen the demise of several characters who had been around for a while and new characters were being added, always a shock to the established on set order that had to be smoothed out both in the script and in real life. There was also talk that Season Four would address the fact that, after three seasons, the zombies had become less terrifying and much more manageable .To that, Norman and the rest of the cast were like carnival barkers, warning that a sense of renewed and unexpected horror from 'The Walkers' would make things "crazier and crazier."

"This season is different," Norman told *The Daily Dead* in a not too veiled attempt at stoking the fires of anticipation in fandom. "It breaths a little differently. You really get to see why some characters step up and fight and why others crumble."

Marc Shapiro

Norman's encounters with the press, at this point, were fairly simple. Like everything else surrounding the new season, there was a sense of familiarity about interviews. The same questions, with rare exception, were being asked and Norman was literally on automatic pilot in answering them, always in an engaging, entertaining, and quotable manner. So it was all good.

Norman acknowledged that playing Daryl as the ultimate outsider over the course of the previous seasons had become a second skin and, in a conversation with *The Daily Dead*, he said he was somewhat taken aback going into Season Four when the producers and writers suggested a change to Daryl's character.

"They pitched to me more of a leadership role and it kind of took me a minute to swallow. Daryl does what he does to keep the camp safe but he's not that [leader] guy. He's still sort of a soldier and he doesn't want the attention of people."

Filming on Season Four continued to be a polished but fairly predictable venture. Lots of sweltering temperatures, lots of long days and nights and an overall vibe that, for Norman, was a daily exercise in the surreal. It was an experience that Norman, on a daily basis, would mentally observe and laugh at with equal relish. "Every day is weird," he joked in a *Travel Channel* interview. "I mean you walk up to the craft services table and there's a zombie sitting there eating a doughnut. It doesn't get any weirder than that."

Easily Norman's most lasting credits after *The Walking Dead* continued to be *The Boondock Saints* movies. They continued to be the little movies that could. Since 2012, the *Boondock* fans were excited when news of a *Boondock Saints III* being in the works broke on the internet. And Norman, for better and worse, helped feed the frenzy. In separate interviews that year Norman was quoted as saying that, first, *Boondock Saints III* was not happening and that he was not interested in doing it if it did. Then he recanted and said *III* was happening and that he was thrilled at the opportunity to play Murphy again. Finally, during a break in filming Season Four, he told a comic book audience that he had not seen a script yet but that he would definitely be interested.

"Never say never."

CHAPTER TWENTY TWO
THANKS AND NO THANKS

Norman had long been aware that his stock was rising in big budget, big studio Hollywood. But reportedly the actor had been picky in such offers and, as always, fitting in big projects around his *The Walking Dead* hiatus was inevitably the deal breaker. But even Norman's total loyalty to the show had to have been tested when an offer from no less a light than George Clooney came his way.

On the surface, *Tomorrowland* seemed the antithesis of what Norman was about. It was being made by Disney, it was rated PG and it would be a mega slam dunk commercial film that would, doubtless, premiere in thousands of theaters and be seen by millions. And the studio wanted Norman to play George Clooney's father in the film.

Norman immediately had an issue with the request as he explained to *Vulture.com*. "With *Tomorrowland* there was an issue about cutting my hair. It was a period film and I would have played the father of George Clooney. But the haircut, the pictures they sent me, it looked like some sort of hair croissant on top of your head. I was like 'How am I going to pull that off?' I have really long, wild guy hair right now and it just wouldn't work."

And the main reason was that there would not be enough time to grow his hair back to normal *Walking Dead* length and he was not about to wear a wig and shortchange the fans of the show. Not surprisingly, Norman's sense of loyalty to *The Walking Dead* won out and he declined the role in *Tomorrowland*.

"This show is my bread and butter," he told *Vulture.com*. "It's my heart. I don't just want to do a giant blockbuster that's going to disappear. I want to do a film that's going to mean something and then I'll go back to my highly watched, super popular television show."

If it sounded as if Norman were being a bit smug, it might well have been with good reason. Whether he cared to admit it or not, going into Season Four of *The Walking Dead*, the actor was feeling quite entrenched and comfortable and, perhaps, a bit entitled. Daryl had risen high enough in *The Walking Dead* popularity polls that there had been veiled threats of riots and fans leaving the show if Daryl were suddenly to become zombie chow. Norman had always played up the notion that 'nobody was safe' and, even though he most likely was, he often exclaimed that he did not want to trumpet his security, lest the writers take it upon themselves to come up with such a good way to kill off Norman that his days might truly be numbered.

In any case, Norman was wrapping up the Season Three and heading for hiatus when he received a phone message that carried a lot more weight than George Clooney. And the cryptic nature of the call, as explained in *Entertainment Weekly*, did not immediately set too well with the actor.

"When we were just about to wrap up the last season, Robert Kirkman left a message saying 'Hey! I really want to talk to you. Can you call me back?' I was like 'Okay. I'm getting the call. I'm gonna die on the show.' So I call Robert back, expecting the worst, and he says 'Hey I'm doing this movie and I want you to be a part of it.' "

As it turned out, Norman, from the moment he had been hired in 2010, had always been in *The Walking Dead* creator's sights. "I don't like to be away from Norman," Kirkman told *Entertainment Weekly*. "It's a problem that I have. So during the off-season, when we're writing scripts for the next season, I go through a thing I call 'Norman Withdrawl.' Anytime I have any kind of projects going on, I'll try and pack it with as much Norman as possible."

Kirkman's offer to Norman seemed fully loaded for Norman, a claustrophobic science fiction thriller called *Air*. Norman stars with Djimon Hounsou in a futuristic, psychological and ultimately terrifying tale of a future in which earth's air has become toxic and two workers in an underground bunker who have been tasked with maintaining the sleeping survivors who will ultimately be revived to help repopulate and bring civilization back. The expected apocalypse tropes are made fresh when it is discovered that one of the two workers has been keeping secrets about a haunted past and plans to implement his own agenda. *Air* was scheduled to begin production right after the conclusion of Season Four of *The Walking Dead* and so, with eight episodes still to be filmed before the end of the season, Norman was looking forward to a first rate diversion.

In the meantime there was still the final episodes of the show to complete and it soon became apparent that *The Walking Dead* was pulling out all the stops in terms of heightened character, deeper levels of horror and enough pure suspense to power a generator.

Norman's enthusiasm was at a fever pitch as he alternately teased and gave vague promises of what was to happen next. These were the moments of pure creative energy that had driven the actor throughout his career and he was like a kid in a candy store with the idea that the role that had finally made him a household name was also the one that was constantly giving him artistic (in an acting sense) the most satisfaction.

For Norman this was something that George Clooney could never have offered.

CHAPTER TWENTY THREE
THANKS FOR THE NICENESS

When Norman interacted with his fans, it was not just another actor being grateful for effect. Norman truly loved the fans and was often amazed at the level of support for himself and his *Walking Dead* alter ego Daryl.

Which was why he accepted and, in a subtle way, encouraged the sketches, paintings and all manner of unusual gifts that, by Season Four, were filling up his house in Georgia, his apartment in New York and, by all accounts, at least a couple production offices and a storage unit or two. "I have closets full of fan art, dolls, blankets, slippers and, I mean, so much stuff," he explained to *SCAD Student Life*.

For Norman, the offerings were heartfelt and personal and he wanted to find a way of rewarding the fans for their love and support. As it would turn out, Norman's initial publishing venture, *The Sun Comes Up...Like a Big Bald Head* had been a huge success and the book's publisher was anxious to follow it up with another photo book. "They were like 'we should do another photo book," Norman told *SCAD Student Life*. "But I did not want to rush. I wanted to let it organically happen. That's when I said 'Let's do a book of the fan art as a proper thank you for the fans who have supported me on the show.'"

Digging through the more than 3000 pieces of fan art to determine which would be in *Thanks For The Niceness* was a labor of love for Norman as well as an insight into just how fandom perceived him. Some of the art pictured him as strong and, occasionally, horrifying while others showed him as being quiet and vulnerable. And then there was the truly 'unusual' offerings, such as the Daryl Dixon cookie with its head depicted as being nearly severed.

As it would turn out, the publication of *Thanks For The Niceness* came within days of the premiere of Season Four of *The Walking Dead* and, if such a thing was possible, the ratings were the highest they had ever been and the critics were falling all over themselves in praise for what they felt was a more mature, equally character and horror driven, chapter in the odyssey. Within a week of Season Four's premiere, AMC greenlighted a Season Five package of 16 new episodes.

Norman's last appearance in Season Four was barely in the can when he was off to film *Air*. True to Kirkman's promise, this would be a tour de force acting turn in which Norman and his co star Djimon Hounsou ran the emotional and psychological gamut in an enclosed and very claustrophobic setting that was shaping up as a throwback to the vibe of the original *Alien*. Of course, this being a Norman vehicle, the chances were good that somebody was going to get hurt during filming. Not surprisingly it would be Norman.

Marc Shapiro

"I broke my toe kicking Djimon," he told *Inside Movies.com*. "I went off on him in a scene and I just started kicking him. I had him hold the bottom of his foot so I could start kicking his foot. But he's so rock hard and made of muscle that I broke my toe when I was doing it. They had to take me to the emergency room in the middle of the night. It was a strange experience."

But as the beginning of production on Season Five of The Walking Dead loomed on the horizon, Norman's schedule continued to fill up. In March 2014, he agreed to co-star in the cops and crooks heist drama *Triple Nine*. It was yet another step up for Norman to be a part of an A list cast that would, most certainly, help raise the actor's career profile. But there was suddenly some concern that *Triple Nine's* filming schedule would coincide with a big chunk of *The Walking Dead's* production and that Daryl might well be conspicuously missing from several episodes. That *Triple Nine* was being filmed in Atlanta helped ease some of the concern, as did the promise that everybody's schedule on the film would be worked out to accommodate other projects.

Season Five of *The Walking Dead* would be a study in contrasts. The first batch of scripts would have the survivors in a gritty, and often zombie-filled, flight in search of sanctuary and a rumored cure for the zombie infestation. The second half of the season would entail the discovery of an idyllic sanctuary called Alexandria and major character conflicts as resolves and flaws bubble over amid the ever present zombies. As expected, new characters would be introduced, a couple would suddenly reappear from earlier season appearances and yes, some characters would die.

Norman stepped right into the mix without skipping a beat. He was intent in going over the early scripts and was quick to suggest things that were not really Daryl be altered. In this by now rock solid collaborative environment, if there had ever been a major blow up, it was never revealed. The mantra of doing whatever it took to make the show better was still going strong.

It was safe to say that by the time Season Five started, Norman may have been the focal point of much of *The Walking Dead's* media coverage, although, in all fairness, other actors had also carved out their own niches of popularity in *The Walking Dead* universe. It was to the ultimate upside of the chemistry of the show, which has never seen a bit of jealousy between cast members reported, real or imagined. Everybody was united, given their own moments to shine and were happy to be a part of a successful show that had rapidly turned into a long running vehicle that, most certainly, was making careers and opening up new opportunities.

For Norman, contemplating Season Five was an emotional victory lap. He continued to be erudite when discussing the ongoing care and feeding of the new season, so much so that people were willing to cut him some slack when his responses to predictable questions, born of lazy journalists, were equally predictable.

But there was also a deeper sense of introspection and thoughtfulness that was permeating his thoughts. In a story that appeared in the archive Norman *Reedus*

Interview Categorized, he responded to the question of Daryl's growing sense of friendliness by remarking "I think Daryl's open to the possibility of being friendly. I don't know if he's full blown friendly yet."

He was also downright philosophical and deep when a reporter for *So It Goes* asked the actor how he felt playing Daryl has affected him as a person. "The character has affected me on so many levels. To be honest, I'm less wild than I used to be. Playing Daryl has really calmed me down as a person and has done wonders for my head. I now appreciate my job as an actor more and I'm a happier person as a result. To have five years to play and build on a character is a rare, rare thing. To have that for five years is kind of amazing."

Norman was, at this point, also feeling freer to talk about his relationship with his son. He knew his son was growing up about the time Mingus turned 15 and began taking his Walking Dead stuff out of his closet and telling his father that he was ready to be his own guy. Norman, with no small amount of parental pride, offered *EA Destination.com* that his son has grown to tolerate and often ignore his father's celebrity.

"He handles it [Norman's fame] really well. Sometimes he actually removes himself from a lot of it on his own. But then he still has to deal with a lot of stuff because of me. I don't really like it when people take my picture when he's with me. He has his own life and it's hard enough being a 15 year-old. But at the end of the day he handles it pretty well.

"Because he's a super smart kid and he's definitely his own person."

CHAPTER TWENTY FOUR
MR. REEDUS GOES TO WASHINGTON

How good was Season Five of *The Walking Dead*? So good that, five days before its official October 12, 2014 unveiling, AMC announced that, yes, there would be a Season Six. The ink was barely dry on the *Variety* announcement when *Walking Dead* fandom was abuzz with alleged spoilers and rumors running amuck. As per usual, who was going to die in the upcoming season was uppermost in the minds of viewers.

And high on the list of potential fatalities was Daryl. Not that anybody was taking that rumor too seriously. 'Daryl will die' had become an annual event in the by now fully entrenched *The Walking Dead* and, at this point, nobody was taking it too seriously. For his part, Norman was much too busy well into 2015 to worry about it too much as he was quite busy during the show's hiatus. He had signed on to play opposite Diane Kruger and Lena Dunham in a road movie/thriller called *Sky*. And the on again/off again *Boondocks Saints III* was apparently on again enough for a start of production date being in the wind and, of course, Norman was all aboard on that one.

Norman also managed to find time to do a couple of music videos for old times sake. In the first for one of his favorite music groups, *Sleater-Kinney*, he actually does a bit of singing while, in a rap music video by *Tricky*, he had some dark and disturbing moments, comforting *Tricky* after arriving at the scene of a murder.

And in an homage to his music video/short film days, Norman took to the desert to direct a music video for the up and coming alternative rock duo *The Bots*. For Norman, this slight creative excursion was a shot to his ingrained work ethic of, more often than not, working without a net. It was basically two musicians, playing in the middle of the desert and then, as he related to *Nerdist.com*, just doing what came naturally. "I loved those dudes," said Norman. "They were up for anything and we kind of worked on the fly, coming up with things as we went along and they had such good ideas."

Anybody who thinks that Norman does not clean up well was in for a pleasant surprise when the actor, with *Saturday Night Live* star Cecily Strong on his arm, was looking all dapper and Prada like as he easily mixed and mingled with celebrities and politicians alike at the annual Washington Correspondents Dinner and showing, as it pertained to his long held aversion to crowds, that he had definitely come out of his shell.

The rumor mill continued to churn as the weeks counted down to the projected May start on filming the new season; with tabloid and gossip writers latching onto any snippet to generate a story. The latest being a report in both *The Wrap* and *International Business Times* that Norman had secretly sold his house in

Palmetto, a sign that he was no longer on the show. In response to *The Wrap*, Norman had a good laugh at denying the story. "That's a total rumor. The house they described is not even my house. Although I wish it was."

As was his want, Norman used his off time to hang out in New York, have quality time with Mingus and hit the occasional comic book or pop culture gatherings. This was nothing but fun. He had grown to love being around what he considered his people, the geeks and TV and horror fanatics that inhabited the fringes of pop culture. He found being around people who were legitimately excited and manic about things that meant something to a relatively small segment of pop culture society, which included himself, to be a jolt of energy to what would occasionally become rote and routine to the actor. And it was during these gatherings that the big topic of conversation would be what was going to happen in Season Six of *The Walking Dead*.

Norman had some tidbits but nothing he could talk about in detail. He teased in the *International Business Times* that "Season Six was going to be epic." He was a bit more specific but not much at hinting at Daryl's place in the Season Six universe. "We know that there are bad guys all around us right now. Daryl knows what kind of people they are…

"…Season Six is going to be a full blown fight."

EPILOGUE
FROM THERE TO HERE

Norman reported to the set of *The Walking Dead* ready to pick up where he left off. But there continued to be storm clouds gathering around the question of whether Daryl would even survive Season Six.

Journalists were digging deep to find the proverbial 'smoking gun' that would have those inclined to bet the farm that Daryl was about to die. The fact that, in 2013, Norman had traded in his reliable agency Don Buchwald & Associates for the more blockbuster/superstar Creative Artists Agency had resulted in Norman suddenly being offered higher profile, more studio inclined films, despite the fact that Norman's choices had largely continued to be based on his whim rather than a slam dunk bottom line.

Of immediate import was the 2015 interview with show creator Robert Kirkman who stated emphatically that, as reported by *Design & Trend*, "A fan favorite was going to die in Season Six." Bottom line, Norman would make it through the first week of filming on the first episode of Season Six in one piece and definitely alive.

But for the future? For Norman it's taken nearly three decades to rise from obscurity to his current station as reigning good guy in the pop culture world. And from there to here he's remained consistent in his dedication to creativity in its purest form in all areas of expression, all the while being maddeningly consistent as a defiant soul, doing things his way, often in the face of logic and economic sense. At a time when true daring is a rarity in this world and creeping conservative attitudes are abroad in the land, Norman, in his own quietly determined way, may well be the bravest of us all.

So the future? For Norman Reedus there will always be a future, set by his own internal clock that runs on heart, soul and a bottom line insistence on doing things his way. By the time you have gotten to this point, Norman, doubtless, will be on to other things. Many other things.

Norman has always insisted that he will be part of *The Walking Dead* as long as the fates allow. But he's a realist as only a creative mind can be. He knows, eventually, that it will be time to go and finally acknowledged that his scenario, for leaving *The Walking Dead* as well as getting on with his life, will be poetically similar.

"I'd rather walk off into the sunset than see Daryl's bloody demise," he told *The Wrap*. "I wouldn't want to die. I'd just want to walk up a hill and, as I get to the top, a little puppy would come out of the woods…

"…And follows me up and over."

FILMOGRAPHY

Owing to the often lengthy intervals between Norman Reedus completing a film and the project actually seeing the light of day, I have chosen to indicate the release date rather than the completion date of the film. In those few cases where the film has not yet been completed, I have indicated where the film is in the post production process.

FILMS

MIMIC (1997)
I'M LOSING YOU (1998)
SIX WAYS TO SUNDAY (1998)
REACH THE ROCK (1998)
DARK HARBOR (1998)
DAVIS IS DEAD (1998)
LET THE DEVIL WEAR BLACK (1999)
8MM (1999)
FLOATING (1999)
THE BOONDOCK SAINTS (1999)
BEAT (2000)
GOSSIP (2000)
BAD SEED (2000)

SAND (2000)
THE BEATNICKS (2001)
LUSTER (2002)
BLADE II (2002)
DEUCES WILD (2002)
NOBODY NEEDS TO KNOW (2003)
TOUGH LUCK (2003)
OCTANE (AKA PULSE) (2003)
UNTIL THE NIGHT (2004)
GREAT WALL, GREAT MEDICINE (2004)
ANTIBODIES (2005)
THE NOTORIOUS BETTIE PAGE (2005)
COMFORTABLY NUMB (2005)
13 GRAVES (2006)
WALLS (2006)
A CRIME (2006)
I THOUGHT OF YOU (2006)
KILLER QUEEN (2006)
AMERICAN GANGSTER (2007)
MOSCOW CHILL (2007)
HERO WANTED (2008)
MEET ME IN BERLIN (2008)
RED CANYON (2008)
DEAD LINE (2008)
CLOWN (2008)
CADILLAC RECORDS (2008)
ECHOES OF EXTINCTION (2008)
STYROFOAM SOUL (2008)
THE CHASE (2009)
MESSENGERS 2: THE SCARECROW (2009)
PANDORUM (2009)
THE BOONDOCK SAINTS II: ALL SAINTS DAY
(2009)

MESKADA (2010)
THE CONSPIRATOR (2010)
OLLIE KLUBLERSHTRUF VS THE NAZIS (2010)
8 UHR 28 (2010)
HELLO HERMAN (2011)
NIGHT OF THE TEMPLAR (2012)
IRON MAN: RISE OF TECHNOVORE (2013)
SUNLIGHT JR. (2013
PAWN SHOP CHRONICLES (2013)
STRETCH (2014)
AIR (2015)
TRIPLE NINE (POST PRODUCTION)
SKY (POST PRODUCTION)

TELEVISION

CHARMED (2003)
MASTERS OF HORROR (2005)
LAW & ORDER: SPECIAL VICTIMS UNIT (2006)
HAWAII FIVE O (2010)
THE WALKING DEAD (2010-PRESENT)

VIDEO GAMES

THE WALKING DEAD: SURVIVAL INSTINCT
(2013)

MUSIC VIDEOS

UGLY KID JOE (1992)
CAT'S IN THE CRADLE
KEITH RICHARDS (1992)
WICKED AS IT SEEMS
BJORK (1994)
VIOLENTLY HAPPY
RADIOHEAD (1995)
FAKE PLASTIC TREES
REM (1995)
STRANGE CURRENCIES
GOO GOO DOLLS (1995)
FLATOP
LADY GAGA (2011)
JUDAS
TRICKY (2014)
SUNDOWN FEATURING TIRAZH
SLEATER KINNEY (2015
NO CITIES NO LOVE

THEATER

MAPS FOR DROWNERS (1991)

SOURCES

I would like to thank the following people for taking the time to share their memories of Norman Reedus' personal and professional life: Carl Lagaspi, Neil Landau, Maura Minsky, Matt Mahurin, Katie Maguire and Michelle Danner.

MAGAZINES

Q, Entertainment Weekly, Rolling Stone, GQ, Elle, Nylon, Men's Journal, Hobo, Complex, Esquire, Lady Gunn, Movieline, Out, Fugue, Content Mode, Vanity Fair, Vanity Fair Italia, NW, Flaunt, YRB, Timeout, SCAD Student Life, So It Goes, Design and Trend.

NEWSPAPERS

The New York Post, The Guardian, The Los Angeles Times, The Sydney Morning Herald, The Stnrd, The Observer, The Daily Mail, The Wall Street Journal, The Village Voice, The Savannah News, The Hollywood Reporter, International Business Times.

WEBSITES

Dixons Vixins.com, WENN.com, Geneology.com, Moose Roots.com, Geneology On Line.com, E!.com,

Imagista.com, Geek On Line.com, The Free
Library.com, Geocities.com, EA Destination.com,
Norman Reedus posterous.com, Icon Vs Icon.com,
Contact Music.com, Youtube.com, Daddyscool.com,
The Suicide Girls.com, Fielding on Film.com,
Tumblur.com, Shock 'Til You Drop.com, Scene B
Seen.com, Dark Reel.com, Cinema Blend.com,
Deadbolt.com, The Desk of Brian.com, Lost In
Reviews.com, A Pathetic Fan Girl.com, It's Just
Movies.com, Digital Spy.com, Comicbookmovie.com,
All in Films.com, Bestmovienews.com, AMC.com,
Deadline.com, Vulture.com, IFC.com, The Daily
Dead.com, IGN.com, Co Create.com, Norman Reedus
Interviews Categorized, Nerdist.com, The Wrap.com.
Texas Divorce Record Index.com, Mocavo.com.

TELEVISION
The View, The Conan O'Brien Show, The Tonight
Show, The Travel Channel.

RADIO
Fan Girl Radio, Dead Dave's Internet Radio.

About the Author

New York Times bestselling author Marc Shapiro has written more than 60 nonfiction celebrity biographies, more than two dozen comic books, numerous short stories and poetry and three short form screenplays. He is also a veteran freelance entertainment journalist.

His young adult book *JK Rowling: The Wizard Behind Harry Potter* was on *The New York Times* bestseller list for four straight weeks. His fact-based book *Total Titanic* was on *The Los Angeles Times* bestseller list for four straight weeks. *Justin Bieber: The Fever* was on the nationwide Canadian bestseller list for several weeks.

Shapiro has written books on such personalities as George Harrison, Carlos Santana, Annette Funicello, Lorde, Lindsay Johan, EL James, Jamie Dornan, Dakota Johnson, Adele and countless others. He also co-authored the autobiography of mixed martial arts fighter Tito Ortiz, *This Is Gonna Hurt: The Life of a Mixed Martial Arts Champion*.

He is currently working on updating his biographies of Gillian Anderson and Lucy Lawless for Riverdale Avenue Books, as well as the first biography of TV-Show genius Shonda Rhimes.

Other Riverdale Avenue Books Titles by Marc Shapiro

The Secret Life of EL James

The Real Steele: The Unauthorized Biography of Dakota Johnson

Inside Grey's Anatomy: The Unauthorized Biography of Jamie Dornan

Annette Funicello: America's Sweetheart

Game: The Resurrection of Tim Tebow

Legally Bieber: Justin Bieber at 18

Lindsay Lohan: Fully Loaded, From Disney to Disaster

Lorde: Your Heroine, How This Young Feminist Broke the Rules and Succeeded

We Love Jenni: An Unauthorized Biography

Who Is Katie Holmes? An Unauthorized Biography

Other titles from Riverdale Avenue Books You Might Like

Dead Sexy:
The Unofficial WALKING DEAD Fan Guide to
Zombie Style, Beauty, Parties
By Paula Conway

Still Hungry for Your Love:
Further Adventures in Zombie Romance
Edited by Lori Perkins

Lightning Source UK Ltd.
Milton Keynes UK
UKOW06f0959131116
287501UK00020B/407/P